READING BETWEEN THE LINES

By **Arnold Brown**, O.C.
Former International Leader
The Salvation Army

Dedicated to the memory of
an admired brother
HENRY
an officer in the Royal Navy

Jesu, Deliverer,
Come Thou to me;
Soothe Thou my voyaging
Over life's sea.
Thou when the storm of death
Roars sweeping by,
Whisper, O Truth of truth,
Peace; it is I.

From the Greek of St. Anatolius

By the same author

- *What Hath God Wrought?*
- *The Gate and the Light*
- *YIN—The Mountain the Wind Blew Here*
- *Fighting for HIS Glory!*
- *The Common People's Gospel*
  (Edited from a translation of the original Japanese)
- *With Christ at the Table*
- *Occupied Manger—Unoccupied Tomb*

ISBN 0-88857-089-9

Printed in Canada
Book Design by R&A Jordan

Contents

Foreword

The wonder of Scripture's inspiration lies in its simplicity of statement as much as in the sweep of its story—from eternity to eternity. Often it is what is left unsaid that stirs most the imagination and allows for a contemporary application of an ancient incident. General Brown masterfully probes the teaching latent in the unmentioned details of the Scripture story, and elicits telling truth for today.

What did Jesus write in the dust with his finger, when a woman taken in the act of adultery was thrown down before Him? Who were the four stretcher-bearers who brought their invalided friend to Jesus? Over what issue, grave or petty, did Euodias and Syntyche fall out? Who made the Cross on which the Saviour died?

This intriguing series of studies surfaces striking lessons on a broad range of issues: integrity in business, the nature of faith, our society's responsibility to its children, the value of silence, the pain of the deaf sealed in a cell of soundlessness, and the paralysing grip of greed upon the soul. This, and much more.

These illuminating meditations reflect General Brown's lifelong fascination with Scripture and his remarkable ability to communicate its truth compellingly. His wide reading, diligent scholarship, and gift for luminous expression are everywhere evident in these brief and readable studies. They will not fail to spark the spiritual imagination and stir the conscience, as well. It is a joy to commend them to the widest possible readership.

Paul A. Rader, (General)

International Headquarters, The Salvation Army, London, England.

Acknowledgments

The threads that are woven into the fabric we call a book usually come from many sources. Some originate in the minds of unknown thinkers and writers, perhaps of another age. Some unspool themselves without effort. Other threads are ravelled, and require time and thought before they can be fitted into the pattern. A few are original and, hopefully, merit inclusion. I am, therefore, indebted to all whose insights helped to make these meditations possible, and hope that they are accurately credited.

Grateful thanks are expressed to General Paul A. Rader, incumbent International Leader of The Salvation Army, for a Foreword which is, in itself, a perceptive précis of the book.

Nurturing production, The Salvation Army's Literature Board at Territorial Headquarters, and Major Ed Forster, Literary Secretary, competently plotted the processes from manuscript to finished article.

With the appreciated encouragement of the Territorial Commander, Commissioner Donald V. Kerr, the book is now available for the inspiration and enjoyment of all who may read it.

Arnold Brown

Introduction

It is assumed that perhaps most of those who will read this little volume will be fairly well acquainted with the Bible itself. For those who are not, scriptural references are given that will lead the reader to the verse or passage from which a comment has been drawn. For example, to some, the name "Hannah" may have little significance. But by turning to the reference given (1 Samuel 1: 27-28), not only will it become obvious as to why her name is included, but an inspiring story of parental love will be discovered.

These reflections do not in any way detract from, or minimize, the scriptural text. They are the result of not only using the eyes to read, but of also using the imagination to do what we sometimes describe as "getting the feel" of something, or when pondering an event "living it out." The book is an attempt to put oneself *into* incidents that happened long ago, much as children do when listening to a story. They become "wrapped up" in it—but in a way that doesn't stop them from interrupting with their questions: "But what about . . . ?" and "Why did he do that?" In their curiosity they so often fasten on the unmentioned.

The noted preacher, the Rev. Dr. David Read, wrote, "I have found in studying the parables that there's sometimes as much to be learned from what Jesus leaves out as from what He describes." To be "unmentioned" is not the same as being "unimportant." To think about some of the omissions, and retrieve them from their silence, can be a profitable learning process. Best of all, it can deepen one's appreciation of the record as it stands.

I had no desire to burden the text with footnotes, annotations, and small-type details of sources. Easy readability was the aim. Scriptural quotations are from various translations but, in the main, from the King James Version. Each chapter stands on its own, and there is no chronological sequence. "Ideally," insisted Raoul Vaneigem, a Belgian philosopher, "a book would have no order to it, and the reader would have to discover his own." That observation is a comfort and an encouragement to this author.

Arnold Brown

Flying Off The Handle

It was a strange happening—the kind that raises eyebrows and makes the skeptic smile. Retold in modern language the story is that a group of seminary students, dissatisfied with their accommodation, asked their superior if they could take some lumber, move nearer the river, and there build a more suitable school. Not only did they get the necessary permission, but the president of the college decided that he would accompany them. When the work began it was realized that more wood than the group had brought was needed, so they began to cut down trees. One of the workers, unfortunately, lost the head of the axe he was using. Separated from its handle it took flight and landed in the river. The worker was doubly upset, and with good cause. Not only was the tool now useless, but, alas, it had been borrowed.

The president of the college, however, was resourceful. He asked to be shown the specific spot where the axe-head had landed in the water. Next, he cut down the branch of a tree and tossed it into the water. Astonishingly, the axe-head at once rose to the surface and floated near enough to the shore for the student to reach out and retrieve it. And there the story ends. Abruptly. No postlude. No moralizing.

The reader can check all this by reading the biblical account in the first six verses of Chapter 6 in the 2nd Book of the Kings (also known as "The Fourth Book of the Kings"). The "seminarians" were from a "School of the Prophets." Such schools in ancient Israel were taught by prophets, and the pupils themselves were regarded as "sons of the prophet." The prophet in this instance was Elisha ("God is Salvation"), whose call to a prophetic ministry had come in a unique way. While engaged in extensive ploughing operations on his wealthy father's estate, the mantle of the revered prophet, Elijah, had been cast on him. This, for Elisha, was unmistakably the call of God, and he answered immediately. His prophetic ministry, covering half a century, was marked by many supernatural happenings, among them the one related here—one which demonstrated in a practical way Elisha's sympathetic nature. He shared the student's embarrassment and distress, and, obviously using his divinely-given power, caused the axe-head to reappear. The miraculous nature of Elisha's action, however, is not stressed.

Today we take floating metal for granted. Supertankers of 500,000 tons crisscross the oceans of the world, and still more massive ships are on the drawing boards. Think of it. Half-a-million tons of metal and cargo riding the surface of the seas as easily as a child's paper boat bobs around the water in his bathtub. (How humans first learned to extract iron from its ores is still debated. In ancient writings iron was often referred to as "the metal of heaven," since it was believed by some to have been obtained from fallen meteors.) It was only in the 19th century that wooden hulls gave way to iron. Those first ships of iron construction were known as "East Indiamen" and were regarded as extraordinary in their size and tonnage. For the people of the time it was hard to believe that a ship of any size made of iron would float at all.

In the report of the floating axe-head, nothing is said about the axe handle. It is *unmentioned*, despite its importance. An axe-head without a handle is not an axe. As far as utility goes it might just as well be at the bottom of the river. In biblical times most wooden handles for implements were made from cedar; cedar imported from Lebanon and considered to be the firmest of all woods. But the joining of handle and axe-head was obviously not a perfect science. Axe-heads seem to have come loose from their handles rather frequently. So often, it seems, that Israel's three Cities of Refuge (the forerunners of today's "safe houses") were established to give protection to, among others, a woodsman whose axe-head had parted from its handle with fatal results. "When a man goeth into the wood . . . to hew wood . . . and the head (of the axe) slippeth from the helve (handle), and lighteth upon his neighbor, that he die; he shall flee unto one of those cities, and live" (Deuteronomy 19:5). Fortunately for the "son" of the prophet Elisha, *his* axe-head had landed in water, and not with deadly result on the head of a brother-student!

It would be a purely academic exercise to argue the respective merits of axe-head and handle. Can one possibly be more important than the other? No, they belong together. The axe-head may get the notoriety, but the unmentioned handle gives the axe-head function and force. Perhaps the colloquial phrase now often heard is not so witless. "Get a handle on it," says the executive to the foreman who has just reported a problem. And when a government project is getting out of control a ministry spokesman will insist, "Of course, we must get a handle on this at once." Executive and spokesman both know that it is "the handle," and the way in which it is wielded, that decides the effectiveness of the cutting edge. When things go flying off in unintended directions, when good intentions (like the axe-head) are drowned, when the precious things we have been lent by life (the axe was borrowed) are allowed to go askew, it is a moment for a supernatural intervention. Thankfully the parts can come together again. Elisha's God (and ours!) is always ready to help us "get a handle" on life, its duties, and its rewards.

The Methuselah Syndrome

Advertising agencies have coined a phrase to describe the over-use of elderly persons in television commercials. They call it "The Methuselah Syndrome."

In advertising, like fashion, there are vogues. One day a style is in. The next, it's out. At one stage youth will be the magic element in sales promotion, whether the product be automobiles or washing machines. Flowing blonde hair, perfectly-proportioned bodies, faultless and brilliantly-white teeth are thought to be essential if the consumer's eye is to be caught and his pocket book emptied. Then comes a U-turn. As one advertising executive has said, "They go straight from the cute 20s to creaky old characters in their late 70s, most wearing wacky clothes." He could have added that next the middle-aged will come into their own, and then, inevitably, it will be back again to youth. Meantime, "Methuselah" reigns.

Not only sellers of merchandise, but most of us ordinary humans have a curious interest in the subject of "age." How often we hear the question: "How old do *you* think she is?" We seem to have our own mental "age-ladder" and we place people on the rung where we think they belong. "Incredible," says our informant, "he's only 35 and already he's a departmental head!" The implication is that he should have been at least 45 to reach such a dignified position. And how did he manage to skip those several age-rungs in his ladder of achievement? It intrigues us to learn that Horatio, Lord Nelson, was only 12 when he joined Britain's Royal Navy and at 22 was a captain. As Admiral of the Fleet he was killed during the Battle of Trafalgar; he was only 47. Other historical figures have defied the age-ladder. Napoleon Bonaparte rose from being 42nd in a class of 58 cadets at the military academy, to being Emperor of the French at the age of 35.

He knew brilliant victories and finally an abysmal defeat. He died at 52. But none of these militarists surpassed Alexander the Great who, three centuries before Christ, swept through country after country like a tearing hurricane to become supreme ruler of an extended empire at the incredibly early age of 32. His consuming ambition was the pursuit of glory and the attainment of divinity, but death claimed him when only 33.

The "Methuselah" epithet is understandable. The Bible says that he lived to the age of 969—longer than anyone else mentioned in Scripture, but not that much longer, comparatively, than many others who were part of the Genesis record. Adam, the first man, lived for 930 years. Noah at the time of the Great Flood was 600 years old, and lived for another 350 years. The Flood was a watershed in many ways. No longer were men to live for almost a millennium. "And the Lord said, My spirit shall not always strive with man, for that he also is flesh: yet his days shall be an hundred and twenty years" (Genesis 6:3). There was an extension for Abraham whose descendants were to be as numberless as the stars (Genesis. 15:5). He was 100 when his son, Isaac, was born, but 75 years later God's Word (Genesis. 15:15) was fulfilled—"And thou shalt go to thy fathers in peace; thou shalt be buried in a good old age." Isaac also was permitted to live beyond the new norm; he was 180 when he "breathed his last and died." Moses, the Emancipator, tells the people, "I am now 120 years old and I am no longer able to lead you," and then climbs to the top of Mount Pisgah. "His eye was not dim, nor his natural force abated" (Deuteronomy. 34:7), but his time had come and God took him, and "no man knoweth his sepulchre to this day "(v.6).

For those interested in knowing at what age this or that happened, the Old Testament is rich in information. For instance, two brothers, Isaac and Esau, were each 40 years of age when they married. Caleb who was sent with Joshua to "spy out the land" seeks an inheritance from Joshua (Joshua 14:6, and following verses) and reminds him that at the time of their dual adventure he was 40 years of age. Now he is 85 and feels "as strong this day as I was in the day that Moses sent me." He gets his wish. In contrast, Eli the Priest (1 Samuel 4), after judging Israel for 40 years, dies of shock at the age of 98. Sitting in his blindness at the wayside, waiting to hear the outcome of the battle with the Philistines, he learns that the Ark of the Covenant has been captured and that both of his sons, as was foretold, have been killed. He falls backward by the side of the gate and his neck, as well as his heart, is broken, " . . . for he was an old man, and heavy . . . " (1 Samuel 4:18).

But how different is the New Testament. References to age are only a handful and all are related to Jesus. Luke tells of a prophetess by the name of Anna (Luke 2:36) who was "a very old woman" when the infant Christ was brought into the temple in Jerusalem to be dedicated. She had been married for seven years, and as a widow for 84 years had prayed and fasted in the temple night and day. Luke also informs us that Jesus was 12 when He held the doctors of the law spellbound with His questions and answers, and that He was "about 30" at the time of His baptism (Luke 3:23). He was derided about His young manhood when He referred to His relationship to Father Abraham. "You're not even 50," they jeered, and started to stone Him (John 8:57).

In paintings depicting the Nativity we see Joseph, Mary's husband, always in the background. He is bearded and often shown with staff in hand. Was he old and needing support? How old *was* he? The jingle-carol says:

> *Saint Joseph was an old man,*
> *And an old man was he,*
> *When he married Mary*
> *In the land of Galilee.*

An apocryphal *History of Joseph* states that he was 93 when betrothed to a 15-year-old Mary, but the statement must surely be written off as fable. Legend also has it that he died at the age of 111 years, when Jesus was 18, but this, too, is conjecture. What we do know is that he was a pious Israelite, that he was a "son of David," that his family belonged to Bethlehem, but that he migrated to Nazareth where he followed the trade of a carpenter. We know that he was a kindly man, that he kept all the observances of the Law, that he was indeed a "father" to Jesus. But nothing is recorded of him during the public ministry of Jesus, and the inference is that he had died before it began. Of his age on that night of nights when shepherds and sages knelt about the manger in which lay his wife's firstborn, we know absolutely nothing.

So much is *unmentioned*. We can only surmise how old Lazarus was when he was restored to life. We know that the widow of

Nain's son, about to be interred when brought back to life by Jesus, was a "young man" (Luke 7:14). But how young? We are not told. How old, we wonder, were the Evangelists when they gave us the Gospels we treasure? Scholars speculate, but none are certain. What was the veteran Apostle Paul's exact age when beheaded in Rome? How old was the exiled John on the Isle of Patmos when granted the apocalyptic vision we now possess in the Book of Revelation? How old was . . . ? Or . . . ? Do we need to know? What matter if such information *is* unrecorded? Philip James Bailey (1816-1902) was right.

> *We live in deeds, not years; in thoughts, not breaths,*
> *In feelings, not in figures on a dial.*
> *We should count time by heart-throbs, He most lives*
> *Who thinks most—feels the noblest—acts the best.*

The Mask of Anonymity

It is a good thing that some names *are* unknown. The cloak of anonymity can mercifully spare relatives or colleagues from undeserved association with dark deeds or wretched scandals. When, for a variety of forensic reasons, court records name suspects only as John or Jane Doe, it is anonymity that is being served, and usefully. On the other hand, it is a pity that some names, names of good and worthy men and women, are unknown, unrecognized and *unmentioned*. The Roman poet, Horace, pointed out that "Many heroes lived before Agamemnon; but all are unknown and unwept, extinguished in everlasting night, because they had no spirited chronicler." Lifting the mask of anonymity we might helpfully learn not only the names of certain individuals, but perhaps come to understand something of their personalities, their lives and their circumstances.

A name means identity. Given or inherited, names distinguish individuals one from another. Often they reveal something about the origins of the family to which a person belongs. We are told that Hubert comes from the early Germanic words *hugu*, "heart," and *berhta*, "bright." (Can we read into this that the first Hubert was a "shining spirit"? Very probably.) Jerome is from the Greek *hieronymos*, "sacred name"; Sarah is from the Hebrew word for "princess"; and Amy is from Old French *amée*, "beloved." Exploring the origins of modern English family names—many of which came into existence in the late Middle Ages—is a fascinating exercise. Some were related to the place of residence or to occupation. Of the dozen most common family names in North America, we are informed, three are occupational (Smith, Miller, Taylor), seven are ancestral (Johnson, Wilson, Anderson, Williams, Jones, Davis, Thomas), one is descriptive

(Brown), and one is a place term (Moore). "A good name is more desirable than great riches" says the Book of Proverbs (22:1). Having a good name should imply blameless character and unfailing integrity.

The Bible is filled with names—familiar names, strange names, and many that we have probably never pronounced accurately. They are the names of all sorts of people, names bestowed to reflect a sense of gratitude, a deeply-held hope, a particular happening, or for still other various reasons. Moses means "drawn forth." The Jewish historian, Josephus, derives the meaning from the Coptic words for "water " and "saved," an allusion to Moses having been found as an infant among the rushes in his tiny, lifesaving coracle. Isaiah means "the salvation of Jehovah." David means "beloved." Daniel means "God is my judge." Esther means "a star." Hannah means "grace" or "prayer." When we familiarize ourselves with the stories of such people, we see how appropriately—and preveniently!—many of them were named.

Names, as well as natures, were changed for some. Simon was renamed Peter, meaning "a rock." Levi was renamed Matthew, meaning "gift of God." The Greek name, Philip, means "lover of horses." (Is there any relationship here to his joining the Ethiopian eunuch, Queen Candace's treasurer, in his horse-drawn chariot—in order to announce the saving grace of God?) Barnabas means "son of consolation." Eunice means "happily victorious." To these examples could be added scores of others from the Scriptures.

But what of the unnamed? What about the anonymous ones? We have only to read the 13th chapter of 1st Kings to realize that some deserve to remain anonymous. It tells of a strange incident during the apostate reign of Jeroboam, and concerns two men—one "the man of God," the other, an aged prophet living in Beth-el. The man of God, coming from a startling confrontation with the king, falls victim to the blandishments of the prophet, and at the end is killed by a lion. It is the sorry story of a lying prophet and a disobedient man of God. Religious history can do without their names!

How different is the story of the woman who touched the hem of Jesus' garment and was healed. Each of the Synoptists record the incident, but do not say who the woman was, or how she contracted the illness that had plagued her for 12 despairing years. Had she seen someone else healed by Jesus, and so came to believe that Jesus could do for her what expensive doctors had been unable to do? We marvel at her faith–"If I only touch . . ." (Matthew 9:21). The record closes on a high note: "The woman was made whole from that hour." And Jesus had His own, gracious way of cancelling out anonymity. Centuries after we still don't know the woman's given name. We know only the lovely name that Jesus gave her—"Daughter."

In one of the astonishing from-death-to-life incidents that occurred during the earthly ministry of Jesus we learn the name of the father (Luke 8:41), but not that of the 12-year-old daughter who was at the centre of the event. Described as "a ruler of the synagogue," Jairus, the father, had well-defined functions; pre-eminently, he was the director of public worship in the synagogue. His fellow-religionists would undoubtedly have derided his seeking help from Jesus, of all people, but concern for his daughter was stronger than any possible criticism. Jairus not only approached Jesus, but "fell at His feet," an act of deference that would shock, and perhaps enrage, his counterparts. Distressed though he was, and knowing that his beloved daughter was *in extremis*, Jairus nevertheless had to wait while the need of another (the woman with the issue of blood) was miraculously met. By then, his daughter had died.

We ask what disease had taken its lethal toll, but there is no answer. Had the girl had a healthy childhood, vigorous in play, ardent in her studies, weaving dreams of adult happiness and usefulness? The record is silent. All we really know is that as an only daughter she was cherished by a distraught father who was willing to put his presidential position at risk in the hope that his daughter might be healed.

A curious mixture of weeping and laughter greeted Jesus and Jairus when they entered the home. The laughter was scornful; it came from those who thought it farcical in the extreme that anything could now be done for the girl, except burial. Tears flowed from the eyes of those who had loved the girl and were now bereaved. Laughter actually increased when Jesus announced that the girl was not dead. "She sleepeth," He said (v.52). Taking her hand, He bade her arise, "And her spirit came again, and she arose straightway" (v.55). No curative or medicinal aid was necessary. There were no incantations or curious rituals—only the word of Jesus and His touch. It is a story full of grace and beauty. For us, the girl is no longer a nonentity, though we are still without knowledge of her given name and the facts of her childhood. Restored to her father and the family, she is now tenderly addressed by Jesus as "My child . . ." No better identification is needed!

Many individuals will forever remain anonymous, but curiosity persists. One speculates about those who were healed by the word and power of Jesus *apart from His presence.* If faith were present, distance was of no consequence. To the Infinite Power space and time are non-existent. But we would like to know the reactions of those who were healed *at a distance.* We know, for example, more about the mother—she was by language and culture a Greek, a Phoenician by descent, and a Syrian by provincial connection—than we do about her miraculously exorcised child who had been tortured by "a vexed spirit" (Matthew 15:21-28; Mark 7:24-30). In the *Clementine Homilies* it is suggested that the mother's name was Justa and the daughter's name Bernice, but Scripture itself does not lift the veil of anonymity.

Parental concern over a son's illness caused a nobleman to contact Jesus in Cana, though the boy himself lay sick in Caesarea (John 4:46-53). The miles between father and son do not matter. The father has faith and it is rewarded. He gets word that incredibly, mysteriously, and at precisely the same moment that Jesus had said, "Thy son liveth," the boy's illness had vanished.

One more illustration. Here is "a servant" (Matthew 8:5-13). Who he was, what his appearance, how clever or inept he may have been, whether he was bond or free, we shall never know. What we do know is that he was valued by his master, and from that we deduce that he must have been a faithful and honest attendant. We do know that he was dreadfully ill with the palsy. His master was a military officer in the Roman army, a *centurion* stationed in Capernaum. That meant he had 100 soldiers under his command. He was probably an attractive specimen of manhood, serious-minded, a leader who carried his badge of office, the vine-rod, with dignity. In asking for his servant to be restored to health there was a distinctive characteristic about the centurion's faith. He was persuaded that a single word of command uttered by Jesus could set in motion forces sufficient for the emergency—just as easily as any command he gave to his own soldiers would be instantly obeyed. In that kind of faith Jesus sees the first fruits of a world redeemed. He is willing to go to the centurion's house, but the centurion, pleading his unworthiness as a host, was certain that a visit was unnecessary. Just a word from Jesus would suffice. And it did! "The servant was healed in that selfsame hour."

Names may be *unmentioned*, circumstances may be *unmentioned*, but as we turn the pages of Scripture we are free, on the basis of whatever facts are available, to use our imagination, and try to enter into the joys and sorrows, the triumphs and the tragedies, the weaknesses and the strengths, the hopes and disappointments, of those upon whom has fallen the mantle of anonymity. The day will come, according to Jesus (Matthew 10:26), when "there is nothing covered, that shall not be revealed; and hid, that shall not be known." Anonymity will be a thing of the past. In the eternal presence of God all believers will be named and known. Identification will be certain, for "*HIS NAME* shall be in their foreheads" (Revelation 22:4).

Questions and Answers

Once in a while there is a television program that combines instruction and entertainment. One such is called *Mastermind*. It came to life in Britain but is now captivating viewers on this side of the Atlantic. The program has that sure-fire ingredient of cliff-hanging suspense, even though its format is incredibly simple. It consists solely of questions and answers. Nothing else. A moderator asks the questions, and contestants strive to answer them. In the first round a competitor can choose a specific subject on which to be questioned—one in which, in all likelihood, he is expert. Thereafter, however, he or she must answer questions that range across the whole spectrum of general knowledge.

"In what year was Peter the Great proclaimed as Emperor of all the Russias?"

"In 1721." Right!

"A famous artist painted the picture entitled, *La Tour Saint Jacques*. What was his name?"

"Utrillo?" Correct!

"And do you know in what year?"

"Possibly 1939." Exactly right!

One is amazed at the amount of information that the human mind can store.

Questions! "It's the Whys? of life," someone has said, "that make us wise." And the Whys? start early. Many parents have been driven to near-distraction by the recurring Whys? of their offspring, even though it is realized that insatiable curiosity is a normal part of a child's mental development. *Inquiringly:* "Why is the sky blue?" "Why don't those big buildings fall down?" *Assertively:* "Why do I have to. . . ?" *Aggressively:* "Why not?" But pity the child who never asks Why? And pity also the adult who has lost the propensity for inquiry! Surely it is the thrust of the Why? that pushes the scientist to new discoveries and new achievements.

Answers! Charles Colton, in *Lacon,* wrote that "The greatest fool may ask more than the wisest man may answer." A serious question deserves a serious answer, even if the answer must be an honest, "I don't know." There are politicians, and others, who seem to be masters of "the invented response." They have an answer for everything. So has the criminal in the dock when examined by the prosecutor, but his self-justifying answers, alas, do not match the polygraph tests. A straightforward honest answer is worth ten thousand evasions.

What questions, we wonder, did the 12-year-old Jesus put to the learned doctors who sat teaching in the temple in Jerusalem? And when questioned by the rabbis, what were the responses He made that caused them to be, as Luke records (2:47), "astonished at His understanding and answers?" As detailed as is "the beloved physician's" record of the life of Jesus, the questions and answers that flowed between this Lad and his religious elders are *unmentioned.* We wish we knew! Great artists have painted the scene—the Lad standing respectfully before the teachers of the law; the faces of the rabbis reflecting wonderment at what they were hearing. But paintings appeal to sight and not to sound. They are mirrors of our own imaginings of the scene, and we are grateful for them. But we wish we had a recording of the discussion that took place that day. What *did* Jesus ask? What *questions* did He answer?

Undoubtedly it was a congenial occasion. The Jewish rabbis rallied the people around the synagogue and the academies of learning, and anyone who was an eager student of the sacred writings would be welcome. Seated, Dean Farrar suggests, in "The Hall of Squares," or in the "Halls of Purchase"—or equally likely in one of the spacious chambers assigned to purposes of teaching which adjoined the Court of the Gentiles—these revered priests and religious teachers would undoubtedly sense the earnest piety of this Boy. He was not lost, as His distraught parents thought. He was where He wanted to be, in the House of God, contemplating spiritual matters, inquiring after eternal truth. Perhaps it was at this very time that He first knew in what direction the road of life would take him. "Thy father and I have sought Thee sorrowing" (2:48), says His mother, Mary. But His reply is on a higher plane. It is His *Heavenly Father* who now commands His loyalty and devotion. It is God the Father's business to which He must now dedicate Himself.

There is only a scant score of years ahead. Three of them will be years of ministry, years filled with questions and answers. Jesus will question and be questioned. He will answer and be answered. The Gadarene demoniac will be asked the simplest of questions, "What is thy name?" Drawing the crowd into the orbit of His teaching, Jesus will ask, "How shall we liken the Kingdom of God? or in what parable shall we set it forth?" (Mark 4:30). His penetrating queries, "Whom do men say that I am?" and "Whom say ye that I am?" are employed to elicit a confession of faith. They result in Peter's declaration, "Thou art the Christ" (Mark 8:27-29). As His earthly life draws to a close Jesus asks a question unlike all that have gone before. It is a question of despair, addressed from the Cross to the Almighty: "My God, My God, why hast Thou forsaken Me?" (Matthew 27:46). Twenty centuries later the question moves us to tears. It is a solemn reminder of the agonizing price paid for our salvation. Thankfully, it is a question that will never be repeated.

Three years of preaching, teaching and healing. Three years filled with framing answers to all sorts of questions in all sorts of situations and circumstances. It is noteworthy that even very ordinary questions unfailingly elicited answers that embodied spiritual teaching. His reply (John 3:1-8) to Nicodemus's question about a second birth ignored the biological difficulty and emphasized the necessity to be born of the Spirit. Some questions Jesus answered *with a question,* encouraging the askers to think a matter through for themselves. When He asked whose superscription was on the coin of the realm, His challengers had a clear and practical answer as to whom their dues should be rendered—to Caesar the things that belong to him, but to God the things that are His (Matthew 22:17-21).

So much for the questions put to our Lord—subtle, shallow, seductive and frequently tempting; others, respectful, sincere, concerned. His answers—forthright, illuminating, sympathetic, stirring the conscience, forgiving and always tender. And the final answer, a Cross.

Quick! The Bandages

He was lying in a ditch, blood oozing from several parts of his body. He had been beaten senseless. But by whom? There was no one else in sight. The place appeared deserted. But the bandits were experts—their technique, "hit hard and hide." It was they who had given this rocky, barren road running down from Jerusalem to Jericho such an evil reputation that it bore the frightening name, "Road of Blood," or "The Bloody Way."

The victim must have been travelling alone. That, in itself, was tempting danger. Most journeyed in companies. To be alone was to provide easy prey for ruthless robbers. These bandits were like eagles circling the sky, scanning the fields for a mindless rabbit or sweeping the shallows for a solitary fish. The descent on the unsuspecting was always swift and vicious.

The victim lay helpless and dying. There were some passers-by, but for various reasons they didn't stop to help—a story in itself. Then a solitary traveller, riding by on his donkey, saw the crumpled, wounded figure in the ditch and stopped to investigate. "If those thieves hadn't gotten this man," he probably said to himself, "I could have been the victim. I'll do what I can." The fact that victim and rescuer lived on opposite sides of a traditional border and held opposite political beliefs didn't matter. There was a life to be saved. Unless the wounds were cleansed and the flow of blood stanched, and quickly, it would be more than a mugging. It would be murder.

Anything like a "911" call belonged to a distant future. Centuries would pass before an ambulance staffed by trained EMTs (emergency medical technicians) and loaded with life-saving equipment—airways for mouth-to-mouth resuscitation, portable artificial ventilation devices, oxygen, suction equipment to vacuum the windpipe and upper digestive tract, a spineboard for cardiac arrest victims, splints, pillows, intravenous kits and certainly what was sorely needed at this moment, lots of bandages—would appear on such a scene. The rescuer wasn't an EMT with 110 hours of classroom and clinical instruction behind him, and he certainly wasn't a physician. What he knew intuitively, however, was that if he didn't wash the man's wounds immediately he would likely die of tetanus.

Fortunately, there was some "oil and wine" in the saddle-bag. Rabbinical writings suggested the use of some kind of vinegar for washing wounds, but if none were handy, and first-aid was vital, then "oil and wine" must suffice. Olives were described as "meat and butter to the peasants," and the oil pressed out of them was a common relish. Fortunately, this good-hearted "paramedic" had some with him!

The bleeding was the chief problem. If it could be stopped and he could get the victim to the next rest-house, the sufferer might survive. If it were a government-run inn there would be nothing to pay because at each stage of the highway there was a supervisor whose duties included not only keeping the road under repair and fixing broken-down vehicles, but also of attending to the needs of travellers. These monitors were salaried by the Roman government and were forbidden to charge a wayfarer for any services rendered. But most likely the inn was one which the rescuer knew, probably one that was privately operated, one whose owner he may have known and where his credit was good. There were many such inns, but, unfortunately, at some of them exorbitant charges were made for each separate provision, the room, the bed, the carpets, the use of a primitive toilet.

The Samaritan had some money. He knew he could give the innkeeper two denarii—two day's earnings—as a deposit, and could settle whatever else was owing on a subsequent visit. But the immediate need was not money; *it was for bandages!* So many things are more important than money, and never more so than in the moment of crisis. A woman passenger on the ill-fated *Titanic* rushes to her stateroom and picks up an orange before running to the lifeboat station. She leaves behind all her jewelry. A man watching the flames billowing from the upstairs windows of his house rushes in to retrieve a treasured photograph. He forgets all about his so-called valuables.

Bandages! Who has bandages? It wasn't as though bandages, though *unmentioned*, were unknown. Even then, the symbol for the ancient occupation of barbering was the striped, red-and-white pole signifying blood and bandages! But, alas, there are no bandages in the saddlebag, medicated or unmedicated. So, off comes the Samaritan's headdress, his khaffiyeh. It's a piece of linen about a yard square, and he rapidly shakes out its folds. Then there is the sound of ripping, of tearing. What had screened his eyes and protected cheekbones and neck from the hot Eastern sun is now strips of cloth—improvised, blood-stanching, life-saving bandages! In his pity for the victim the rescuer will even risk a sunstroke!

So "he bound up his wounds . . . "

Did it really happen like this? We don't know, because it's only a story, a story told by Jesus (Luke 10:25-37), told to instruct a lawyer who was mcre interested in controversy than compassion, and who needed to learn the real meaning of "loving one's neighbor as oneself." When the supercilious solicitor asks the question, "And who is my neighbor?" Jesus tells him about this man "who fell among thieves" and who was robbed, beaten and left half-dead. Happily, the victim is saved from death by a member of an ostracized race who *doesn't* "pass him by on the other side." Now the lawyer is snared in his own trap. He is forced to admit before the entire synagogue congregation that good neighborliness is not restricted to one's own kith or clan. It is compassion in action, turned loose on anyone who lies helpless and bleeding in the ditches of life. It has nothing to do with nationality but everything to do with need!

As a result, Helmut Thielike suggests, the decisive question is not: "Who is my neighbor?" but "To whom am I a neighbor; where am I required?" It may be that there is someone, somewhere, who is pinning his hopes on me, desperately hoping that I will not pass by on the other side. Beaten by life, half-dead with misgivings and fear, I am his only hope of rescue. Am I ready to shed, and to shred, my precious kaffiyeh? As Luther put it: "To whom am I to be Christ?"

A Clean Sweep

Lots of people lose lots of things. If you want evidence read the "Lost and Found" column of any community newspaper. Here, for instance, is a pathetic advertisement pleading for the return of a lost kitten: color, marmalade; has a bent tail; answers to the name of Apollo ("Polly" for short). More sentimental still is a notice that someone has lost a treasured gold locket. It is priceless because in it is a lock of "his" hair. Incredibly, someone (is it with tongue in cheek?) is asking for help in finding a lost set of false teeth. Reading such items one is sadly aware that much more valuable, indeed the most valuable, things in life can be lost without any effort at all being made for their return. Have we ever seen in a "Lost and Found" column a businessman's plea for the return of lost honesty, a young woman's cry for the return of lost purity, or someone's desperate appeal for the return of a lost soul? Too many, if totally sincere, would have to whisper, "I—I think we are lost!" as did the young German soldier, battered and confused by the chaos of the battlefield, described in Erich Maria Remarque's dramatic novel, *All Quiet on the Western Front*.

The Bible has a "Lost and Found" column of its own in the 15th Chapter of Luke. Jesus, more than any other person who has lived on this earth, knew about real "lostness." His concern was for a lost humanity; a humanity that needed to find God and be found of Him. His mission and His passion were declared in the words, "The Son of man is come to seek and to save that which was lost" (Luke 19:10). He knew that being spiritually lost could be a bewildering experience, and He illustrated it by telling about a sheep that strayed from the fold but could not find its way back.

He also knew that to be spiritually lost could mean

humiliation and heartbreak, and to emphasize the fact he told the story of a son who went missing in "a far country" and was lost to purity and human dignity. Jesus capped the story by telling of the father's rapture when "the lost was found," just as God Himself rejoices when lost sinners find forgiveness and an eternal home for the soul.

Included in the Gospel's "Lost and Found column" is also the story of a lost coin. No one likes to lose money. Most would rather give it away than lose it. Losing money, it seems, has a curiously disturbing effect on the loser. Television commercials succeed in vividly portraying the panic, the hysteria, of the man who loses his traveller's cheques when away from home. In the story told by Jesus the money-loser was a woman. She had ten silver coins, but somehow one got lost, and judging by her reaction the loss was significant. Perhaps there was a family to be fed, and every bit of money was needed in order to provide enough food. Perhaps there was a husband whose bad temper was to be feared, and who, when he learned of the loss, would accuse her of arrant carelessness and beat her.

The value of the coin the woman lost can only be guessed. In Palestine, at the time, there were actually two kinds of currency. One comprised the gold and silver coins issued by decree of the Emperor who authoritatively controlled the minting of them. Emperor Vespasian, for example, authorized a coin sometime after AD 70 that carried the suggestive inscription, *Judaea Capta*, and the picture of a palm tree. One side depicts a male Jew in fetters; on the other is a Jewish woman in mourning. But the Roman authorities also tolerated what might be called "local currency," negotiable only within the boundaries of certain provinces or municipalities. Whether the woman's ten silver coins were federal or municipal they were obviously valuable to her, otherwise she would not have looked with such energy and diligence for the one that was missing.

She did two things. First, she lit a lamp. Secondly, she "swept the house." The first explains itself. It may have been night, and without some illumination a search would be impossible. Or perhaps it was just that there were some shadowy corners, or dark places under the larger pieces of furniture, and hopefully, when the lamplight fell on it the lost coin would reflect the beam and be revealed. Probably the woman used a portable lamp as she went from room to room. Portable lamps were in common use, and handy. When not carried, they could be suspended from a bracket that either hung from the ceiling or was fixed to a wall.

But why did the woman "sweep *the house*"? Perhaps she wasn't sure in which room she had lost her piece of silver, though in the poorer type of houses of the time there were not all that many "rooms." Most houses were of one-storey construction—big, square, box-like apartments. Often they were divided into two parts, not by a wall, but by one section being on a higher level than the other. On the upper part would be the beds, the clothes chests, and sometimes the cooking utensils. But to sweep, one must have something to sweep with. We would have expected the record to read, "She took a lamp and *with a broom* swept all the rooms of the house." But the broom is not mentioned. Its availability is taken for granted. A lamp is important: "It giveth light to all who are in the house." But a broom? Useful, of course, but too common to mention? Kept in a closet or cupboard it quietly awaits its moment of service. But when a coin goes missing it is the common broom that becomes a necessity and is all-important. It is the humble broom that will sweep the lost coin out of its hiding place, and when it does, a distraught woman's life will once again be livable.

Interestingly, the broom is a direct gift of nature. It is usually made from a member of the grass family called *sorghum* which originated in the Middle East, in Syria. One of *sorghum's* four main groups is "broom corn," and for centuries the plant has provided the fibres that are used to make brooms. Very early each morning armies of sweepers move out into the streets of the great cities of the Middle East, the Far East, the sub-continent of India, and elsewhere, broom in hand. The brooms they use are essentially the same as the one that saved the sanity of the woman who "swept the house" and who searched until she found the lost coin.

What was it that Jesus wanted His hearers to draw from His telling of such a commonplace, everyday incident? Surely it was that everyone is a creature of absolute worth in God's economy, and that God, in love, never gives up seeking the lost soul. His light penetrates the shades of fear and failure. It shines into the darkest corners of the soul with mercy and with hope. It irradiates the fog of helplessness and despair. Perhaps we should rename the story, and call it "the parable of the *found* coin."

Nor should we forget the humble broom. Being unmentioned does not mean being unimportant!

The Green-eyed Monster

In the parable Jesus told about "a prodigal son" and his homecoming (Luke 15:11-32), the *dramatis personae* included several humans and, as well, two animals. On the human side there was a father and his two sons, and there were also servants. The animals were a calf and a kid, and it was the slaughtering of the calf that triggered the elder son's bitter tirade against his father.

One gets the impression that the elder brother had worked uncomplainingly to make the farm productive. He was evidently still toiling "in the field" when the prodigal's return was already being celebrated. Obviously he had a sense of responsibility for the estate that his younger brother lacked. The younger lad's intention had been to leave the homestead as soon as he could. He ached for the freedom to do what he wanted, where he wanted, and when he wanted. Not for him the claims of barn or field! He was fed up with the monotony of it all. To rise before the sun, to toil all day in all kinds of weather, and then to sink exhausted into bed knowing that the next day would mean the same deadening routine, made him resentful and restless. His dreams were of the glamorous city where beautiful women were anxious for his company; where an "early to bed and early to rise" way of life would be forgotten and be replaced by lavish banqueting and midnight frolicking.

Nor was he prepared to wait for his father to die before getting his share of the inheritance. He wanted his patrimony now, now while exciting thoughts of life in "the city" fired his imagination and stimulated his passions. The father, perhaps with reluctance, gave him the portion to which he was entitled, and the young adventurer immediately turned his back on the family home and left for "a far country." So far as the maintenance of the farm was concerned his attitude, in modern parlance, was, "Let George do it."

Weeks became months. The seasons came and went. Sowing led to reaping and long hours on the threshing floor. Blossoms became fruit and the toil of harvesting followed. There was the livestock to be managed and kept free of disease. Negligence could mean the ruination of the herd and lead to poverty. Proper breeding was vital, and the elder brother waited impatiently, one can imagine, for the arrival of one particular calf. The pregnant dam was a prize animal. Gestation had been normal. The offspring, when it arrived, could be a perfect and valuable asset.

When the moment of delivery actually came, the elder brother was there. Perhaps it was after midnight when, in the darkness, he ploughed through the mud towards the barn, hurrying faster as the cow's labor moans grew louder. This was not a new experience for him. He was used to helping in the birth of animals, and was expert at it. But there was something extraordinary about this birth. It was different and special. A prize cow was producing a superior calf and he believed that it would be rightfully his, and his alone. He would tend the animal with particular care. It would have proper forage, *lucerne* (similar to the alfalfa of our day), which was widely used in New Testament times in the production of lean meat.

Carefully nurtured, the calf became the senior brother's pride and joy. Its development did credit to his capable husbandry. A pity that his junior brother couldn't have had something as valuable to show for his handiwork! But at that moment the prodigal's whereabouts were unknown, though the elder brother was sure that his father had made many attempts to find him. If the prodigal's location and situation had been known, would the elder brother have been worried, dismayed, or just uninterested? Probably the latter. Not so the father. From the story told by Jesus we know that the father was heartbroken. He was constantly peering into the distance, wondering when, if ever, the figure he longed to see would appear around that distant bend where the road twisted out of sight.

When it did happen, it was a chastened penitent who dragged himself with apprehensive steps towards his father and home. His sojourn in the far country had ended disastrously. His popularity had vanished when his money ran out. To worsen matters, the "far country's" economy had collapsed and famine had swept the land. Though he was the son of a prosperous landowner he had been forced to live with swine and eat the same food in order to stay alive. When he "came to himself" it was like waking from a nightmare or emerging from a coma. The contrast between his earlier home life and his present degradation overwhelmed him. The thought of it was soul-shaking. He realized his boneheadedness, his utter stupidity, the dishonor he had brought on his family and his own ignominy. Father and home were his only hope. He would "arise and go." Farewell to the pigsty. Thank God for a home to go to!

The actual homecoming is described in detail—the joy of the father racing to bestow the embrace of welcome and the kiss of forgiveness. A robe replaces the rags of the swineherd. Sandals are placed on the bare, lacerated feet. A ring is slipped on to the finger signalling a return to sonship. The father orders a celebratory feast: "Bring forth the fatted calf." Let joy be unconfined. All in the house will eat, drink and be merry. And shining through the parable is the truth that "joy shall be in heaven over one sinner that repenteth" (Luke 15:7).

But wait a moment. The fatted calf? The elder brother's pride and joy. Is it to be sacrificed in honor of a wilful, wayward son's return? The elder brother had not been given even a kid so that he might gather his friends together and mount a feast. A young goat and a fatted calf? Absolutely no comparison! We are not told whether or not the father's placating, generous words, "All that I have is thine," calmed the elder son's temper? We wish we knew, but it is *unmentioned*. Did he storm back to the field in anger, his soul in the grip of "the green-eyed monster" we call jealousy? Or did he, as we would hope, concede that his father was right; that when a wanderer returns, when the lost is found, when one thought dead is actually alive, a feast is abundantly merited. If he did, it remains *unmentioned*.

And, after all, the fatted calf *did* belong to the father!

The Missing Bucket

Think of it. You have had a long journey, on foot. It is noon and the sun is at its hottest. You are sitting, parched and thirsting, on the stone parapet surrounding a well that is reputed to have the clearest and most revivifying water in the whole of the countryside. But there is a problem. You have nothing with which to draw the water—no cup, no jug, no pitcher, nothing. Not even a primitive dipper made, as was customary for the people of biblical times, from the hard shell of a gourd. The problem is compounded because this particular well is deep, more than 100-feet deep, and the water is unobtainable unless a container of some kind is attached to a rope and lowered. (Present-day tourists take a cup of water and empty it into this ancient well. They are surprised by the long interval of silence before the sound of the water from the cup is heard splashing on to the surface of the water below.)

This was the situation in which Jesus found Himself as He rested wearily beside Jacob's Well (John 4:1-24), dug centuries before and bequeathed by the patriarch to his favorite son, Joseph, whose burial site is close by. It was still providing water for those who lived in the Samaritan town of Sychar, under the shadow of Mount Gerizim, as well as for any needy passer-by like Jesus.

At the well Jesus was joined by a woman who had come to draw water. When He asked her for a drink He got a baldly pragmatic reply: "Thou hast nothing to draw with" (v.11). Was it simply a throw-away observation? Or, was it, in view of the tribal hostility between Jews and Samaritans a scornful comment. Admittedly, the circumstance was unusual. Travellers of the time usually carried with them some kind of water jug, some kind of flask. Not so Jesus on this occasion. Perhaps the disciples travelling with

Him might have had some sort of container with them, but they had gone into the neighboring city to buy what was necessary for their simple wants.

The woman herself would certainly have had some sort of water-jug with her seeing she had come to the well for the very purpose of drawing water. Could she not have loaned it to Jesus? The problem would have been solved immediately. But ritual differences were involved here. "For Jews do not associate with the Samaritans" (v.9). But what or whom, we wonder, would have been "unclean" had the lips of Jesus touched the rim of the woman's waterpot?

Regional and ritual differences apart, all would have been well had not one simple item been missing—the bucket which normally was to be found at every well. Traditionally one was left as a convenience for those who, like Jesus, had no container of their own. To "die of thirst" was more than a cliché. Thirst could be intense in the hottest time of the year—a distress viewed so sympathetically that a Jew, forbidden to speak in public to a woman, even to his wife, *was* permitted under Rabbinical rule to ask a woman for a drink.

"Water in the East is not only a necessity, but a delicious luxury, and Palestinians are connoisseurs as to its quality," wrote one biblical expositor. Water from Jacob's Well had what its users called a "lightness" in comparison with the lime-induced hardness of water from other nearby sources. Translators have pointed out that, according to the Greek text, the Samaritan woman from whom Jesus requested a drink of water called the well a "cistern, or pit." She was right; it is not a well of living water, a spring or a fountain, but rather a cistern intended to hold water. The true mouth of the cistern is several feet below the surface, and is just wide enough for a man to enter. Lower down the cistern broadens out into a wider and, as already mentioned, an exceedingly deep cylinder. Early authorities established that the water in it was replenished mainly by rainfall and by a natural percolation through the masonry that to this day lines the interior. The water, according to G. A. Smith's *Historical Geography of the Holy Land*, was "cool, palatable and refreshing."

All interesting, but of faint interest to someone dehydrated, fatigued, and under spiritual stress. To peer into the depths of the cistern and actually see the cool water, and yet be unable to reach it, would surely multiply both the craving and the need for it. Jesus Himself told the story of a rich man who indulged himself in food and finery but ignored the plight of a diseased beggar at his gate. Death and judgment, however, reversed the roles, and from the place of eternal banishment the rich man pleaded that the beggar be allowed to "dip the tip of his finger in water, and cool my tongue" (Luke 16:24). I recall explaining to the woman governor of the important State of Kerala, situated at the south-western tip of the sub-continent of India that, in view of the extensive needs of the people, everything we were doing seemed like "a drop in the bucket." "Perhaps," she replied, "but remember, every drop is a pearl." Dives would have thought so!

No bucket meant no water. Samuel Woodworth, recalling in verse the scenes of his childhood, wrote of "The old oaken bucket, the iron-bound bucket, the moss-covered bucket which hung in the well." What counted was not its size or shape, its appearance or its age, but its availability, its function. Sam Walter Foss, who gave us the memorable line, "I shall not pass this way again . . ." expressed the difference the lowly bucket could make to sailors who knew that at last "they sailed upon the broad mouth of the Amazon":

> A voice came o'er the waters far,
> "Just drop your bucket where you are."
> And then they dipped and drank their fill
> Of waters fresh from mead and hill.

At Jacob's Well the bucket is *unmentioned* because it was missing! We leave the story without knowing whether Jesus did or did not have a drink of water. Bucket, or no bucket, we feel that the ending would have been the same—a bewildered woman transformed into a working missionary, and a two-day teaching stay among townspeople who sensed that the Lord of life, with an eternal message, was actually in their midst.

But there is "the parable of the missing bucket," and it should remind us that, whoever we are, however lowly our station or function, we should never be missing from our place of Christian duty and commitment.

CHAPTER 9

The Ubiquitous Basket

The teachings of Jesus sparkled with telling illustrations. By relating a simple incident, or telling a story that everyone could understand, He created windows through which His hearers could glimpse profound truths. The parables told by Jesus were not, Dr. Harold A. Bosley suggests in his book, *He Spoke to Them in Parables,* inspired utterances of the prophet streaked with denunciation and high emotion, but rather "quiet conversations—a teacher explaining a point to a listener."

One would expect Jesus to know what he was talking about when illustratively He spoke of the cost of building a house, or the necessity for laying a firm foundation, or the requirement that a barn must be of the right size to hold what had to be stored in it. After all, He had been a carpenter. But He could also pluck graphic illustrations from various other aspects of daily life. Carpentry could not have been His only interest. He was not a fisherman, but twice He told experienced but unsuccessful fishermen where the catch was to be found, and, actually, how to land it. No wonder they knew exactly what He meant when He told them they must be "fishers of men." They would have to go where a "catch" was possible, have the right "bait," and toil without ceasing whether the climate was compatible or not. Nor was He a botanist, but He knew when a fig tree should bear fruit, and He could appreciate the beauty of the lilies of the field. Through His illustrations He dealt with the nastiness of hypocrisy, or the providential interest of a caring God in the smallest details of people's lives.

Three of the four Gospels record the illustration used by Jesus about the farmer sowing the seed (Matthew 13:3-9, Mark 4:3-9, Luke 8:5-18). Matthew paints a picture for us. Jesus is in a boat offshore.

From this unusual pulpit He could see the growing crowd of people "coming . . .from town after town" (Luke 8:4) and lining the water's edge. Also He himself could easily be seen and heard. In choosing this illustration Jesus may have been speaking reflectively of the difficulties and disappointments He himself was encountering in preaching about the Kingdom of God, and warning that it would be the same for all would-be heralds of God's saving grace. It is not the fault of the seed, or of the sower, Jesus explains, that the vital germ or grain of the plant may fail to germinate. The results depend upon the promising or unpromising nature of the ground on which it chances to fall. Nevertheless the sower must do his work. If some of the seed fails, his function is not negated. The teaching, Jesus implies, must be imparted. The Word must be trusted to do its work in congenial hearts.

The artless introduction to the story, "A farmer went out to sow his seed" would immediately conjure up a familiar picture for His hearers. Sowing was generally done by hand. Pliny mentions that the sower had to drill himself so that his hand kept time with his stride, in order that he might scatter the seed with proper uniformity. In the recording of the illustration something is taken for granted and *unmentioned*. The seed would be carried by the sower, but how? Preacher and congregation, all present, would know the answer. The seed was carried in a basket—a simple wicker basket skilfully woven together in a way refined by centuries of practice. So we discover an *unmentioned* but absolutely necessary utility—the lowly, unobtrusive basket! Without her basket how could the laundress manage? Or the fruiterer with his apples? Or the sower with his seed?

Basketry is one of the oldest and most widespread of handicrafts. Foraging peoples of earliest times needed lightweight receptacles in which to carry food and water. Using whatever materials were available—leather, porcupine quills, whale bone, bamboo, rattan or cane, or the plentiful willow reeds that flourished in the marshlands—basketry was born. Through the millennia the craft has persisted in places as far apart as Peru and the Nile Valley.

Basketry has its place in the literature of the Bible. The term, "bread basket," came into use when the baker told Joseph of his dream in which he carried three baskets of bread on his head (Genesis 40:16). And what about that basket found floating in the Nile, a basket that was providing a "safe house" for the infant Moses? (Exodus 2:5).

Baskets were part of the symbolism when Jeremiah, in his vision (Jeremiah 24:1), sees two baskets of figs in front of the Temple of the Lord and is reminded of the difference between good and evil. One basket contains wholesome fruit; the fruit in the other is rotten and inedible. The prophet Amos has an almost identical vision (Amos 8:2). He sees a basket of ripe fruit conveying the dire message that "the time is ripe" for divine judgment. In Zechariah's strange vision (Zechariah 5:6), the prophet is stunned to see a measuring basket (an *ephah*) descending from the heavens, and when the lid is raised there is a woman inside, the personification of sinfulness. The heavy lid is immediately replaced and the basket, with its loathsome occupant, is borne aloft and away by two creatures with the wind in their wings.

There are also references to baskets in the New Testament. When Jesus likened the Kingdom of Heaven to a net full of fish, He went on to say that the good fish were placed in a basket, but that the bad were thrown away. It was a solemn reminder that judgment was inescapable, and that good and evil went to separate destinations (Matthew 13:49). After the feeding of the five thousand, when five loaves and two small fishes were miraculously multiplied, the lowly basket again came into its own. No fewer than 12 baskets were required to collect the broken pieces of food that were left over (Matthew 14:20). In the feeding of the four thousand, however, the baskets (Mark 8:8) are described in the Greek by a different word. Probably, scholars think, because there was a difference in the baskets used, either in size, shape, or in the material from which they were made. In biblical times, as today, there were baskets of all shapes and sizes—small, decorative fruit baskets at the centre of the table; larger baskets, filled with provisions, that the women balanced on their heads; and some large enough to provide a hiding place for a hunted man.

One such basket, fortunately for the Christian Church, saved the Apostle Paul's life. In Damascus, in the early days of his ministry, and while his credibility as an "apostle" was still under scrutiny, Saul, as he was then known, became the object of dangerous hostility. It was a basket that made possible his escape. In it, and by night, he was lowered to the ground through an opening in the wall.

But now, back to the sower and the seed. That a basket was needed to hold the seed was self-evident. Sowing in biblical times was mostly by hand, and then the grain was sometimes raked in and sometimes ploughed in. But it was from what was generally known as a "three-peck" basket that the seed was grasped by the handful and then skilfully scattered. The "peck" as a measurement of quantity was a fourth of a bushel, 8 quarts, or 8.8 litres. For the mathematically interested, it meant that the average basket had a capacity of 1,612.815 cubic inches. To the sower it simply meant a heavy load strapped against the chest, a load that was renewed again and again as the sowing proceeded.

Mentioned or unmentioned, the basket was, and still is, a necessity. It holds things, important things like seed, some of which, hopefully, as Jesus said, may fall "on good soil"—soil which "stands for those with a noble and good heart, who hear the word, retain it, and by persevering produce a crop" (Luke 8:15 NIV). Jesus said that "the seed is the word of God." His followers, then, must be "carriers" of that seed, of that Word which, for the receptive heart, will mean hope and blessing, comfort and direction, and, best of all, in and through Christ, eternal salvation.

Blessed be the lowly basket! And much-blessed be all who faithfully carry the seed of the Word!

CHAPTER 10

"The Moving Finger Writes"

It was a child's question, posed in all innocence. The Sunday school teacher had told the children that only once, according to the Bible, did Jesus write anything, and she had described the occasion in detail. "But why," asked the child, "did Jesus have to use His finger to write? Didn't He have a pen or a pencil?"

The simple answer would be, "No. When Jesus was on earth pens and pencils had not been invented." Centuries would pass before writing instruments as we know them today would be common. The humble pencil, for example, is the result of involved processes that were unknown to our forebears—how powdered graphite, clay and water are blended and then extruded into small-diameter rods, dried and kiln-fired at high temperatures beyond 1000°F; how the "lead" rods are then inserted into the wooden holders, the wood having been specially selected for its grain and texture.

Jesus would, however, have been quite familiar with the writing instruments of His day. The Greeks and Romans used a metal stylus to write on waxed tablets. These sharp-pointed instruments cut into a thin film of wax, usually black, that was spread over a wooden tablet, according to A. C. Bouquet in his book, *Everyday Life in New Testament Times.* The effect would resemble the "reverse" lettering now so easily produced on a modern computer—white wording on a black background. The blunt end of the stylus was used to erase the markings. The tablets themselves could be used time and time again simply by heating and wiping away the molten wax. Jewish scribes also used reed pens, sharpened with a knife in the same way as the old-fashioned quill pen. Various kinds of ink were used, but perhaps the most common was made from soot collected from a marble furnace in which pitch pine was burnt. The soot was then mixed with glue or vinegar, dried in the sun, and formed into blocks.

But styluses (and pens and pencils) have little to do with what this one and only "writing incident" is really about (John 8:1-11). If Jesus had needed a stylus, undoubtedly one would have been forthcoming. Financial records were probably kept by Judas, and possibly he would have had one in his possession.

Picture the scene. It occurs in the final year of our Lord's earthly ministry—"The Year of Opposition." Not only was He being harassed at every turn, He was now continually living under the threat of death. At the time of this episode the chief priests and the Pharisees were exceedingly annoyed with the Temple police who seemed to have fallen under the spell of Jesus and had failed to arrest Him. Calm and undaunted, at daybreak Jesus returns to the Temple and resumes His teaching. The crowd is responsive and gathers closely around Him. Suddenly, there is an intrusion. A group comprising doctors of the law and Pharisees drag a woman into the centre of the crowd, and one can imagine her screaming and protests as she struggles with her captors. Have her accusers forgotten that they are in the Temple, in *God's* house, a place dedicated to worship and teaching, and certainly not to commotion and irreverence? But evidently these brazen religionists couldn't care less. They are sure that at last they have successfully snared their prey, and that Jesus, whatever He says, will be condemned out of His own mouth.

Cynically, they address Jesus as, "Master." They tell Him that the woman has been caught in the act of adultery and remind Him, (unnecessarily!) that the law of Moses decrees death by stoning for such flagrant misconduct. Does Jesus agree? Any comment He makes, they think, will convict Him, and they wait for His response with bated breath. But it is a mischievous trick, and Jesus knows it.

Centuries before, the finger of a man's hand had written a message of condemnation on the wall of King Belshazzar's palace (Daniel 5:1-6). In the midst of a riotous feast during which the sacred vessels of the Temple had been profanely used, the terrified monarch, his knees knocking with fear, heard the word of judgment: "Full weight you should be; light weight you are; divided weight you shall be" Belshazzar is told that he has been "weighed in the balances and found wanting" (v.27). Now, the finger of God writes again. Jesus, sickened by the knavery of His tempters, and feeling deep compassion for the woman who has sinned, is silent. As though He wants to shut out the very sight of these smug, self-styled moralists, He bows towards the ground, and traces something in the dust.

What He wrote is unmentioned. Characters? Words? Sentences? No one knows. With the woman's denouncers in mind it could appropriately have been, "Weighed in the balances and found wanting." But whatever He wrote, the Perfect Man had the perfect answer. "Yes. Fulfil the law of Moses, but let him that is without sin cast the first stone." Once again He stoops and writes in the dust. Again there is no clue as to what He wrote. As a verdict on blatant hypocrisy it could well have been, "Thy kingdom is divided." But it is idle to conjecture what the Master wrote that day. It is the action, and nothing else, that is significant, says J. Moffat in *The Dictionary of Christ and the Gospels.*

When Jesus straightened and looked about Him there were no longer any accusers, just an enthralled crowd and a trembling woman who hears the word of liberation—"Go!"—and who also hears the word of pardon—"Neither do I condemn thee." There is also a gracious, never-to-be-forgotten word of spiritual instruction—"Do not sin again!"

CHAPTER 11

Clouds of Glory

We turn away from the television screen sickened by the images of wounded, naked, and cruelly abandoned infants and children—a pernicious side effect of a useless war. We crumple the page of our newspaper and throw it away, unsettled by the photograph of undernourished babies stuffed into a suffocatingly crowded orphanage. A magazine displays a tragedy in living color—the death of two fresh-faced infants. Their mother, pandering to the demands of a lover, fastens them in the family car and lets it take them to a watery grave. The radio repeats, on the hour every hour, the crime of a man and woman who do not deserve to be called parents. They anchored their helpless offspring to the bed, beat him until he was black and blue, and then starved him to death. And all aspects of the mass media unite, it seems, in disseminating shameful, horrific stories of child abuse—abuse so incredibly degenerate that the animal kingdom, if it could comprehend the evil, would wonder what the words "human" and its derivative, "humane," really mean.

Against this "inhuman" background we set the words of the English poet, William Wordsworth—lines from verses that many consider to be his greatest lyrical achievement, *Ode: Intimations of Immortality.*

> *But trailing clouds of glory do we come*
> *From God, who is our home:*
> *Heaven lies about us in our infancy.*

The poet sees what many miss, for it is still true, despite everything stated in the preceding paragraph, that every infant coming from "out of the everywhere into here" brings with him clouds of glory and a hint of Heaven. It is not the child's fault that all too often the "trailing clouds" of promise and potential evaporate. The barbarian's wickedness and the exploiter's sadism are to blame.

"Jesus," wrote Shailer Matthews in *The Social Teachings of Jesus*, "lifted to a new plane our whole conception of children." All society, he felt, could be regenerated by a Christian emphasis on the family and family life. Christ's emphasis on the institution of the family was extraordinary—and that without establishing regulations governing the behavior of parents and children. He had, of course, His own protected childhood to remember—with a mother whose love lasted to the end of His life, and a father who taught Him to excel in His trade. As well, He would be aware of the long tradition of Jewish family life in which high value was set upon the possession of children. "Like the olive-branches round about thy table; lo thus shall the man be blessed that feareth Yahweh."

Knowledge of the Hebrew Scriptures would be a natural part of Christ's inheritance. He knew that He Himself was the Child of whom Isaiah had prophesied—the Child who would be "the Prince of Peace" (9:6). He would have read that tender reference in the Book of Ruth 4:16 NIV : "Naomi took the child, laid him in her lap and cared for him." That child, Obed, was to be the grandfather of King David, a direct ancestor of Jesus Himself. In the Jewish home the sickness of a child was cause for anxiety, and death caused great grief, "with lamentations and wailing." We read of David's anguish when his son, illegitimately conceived by Uriah's wife, Bathsheba, fell ill exactly as Nathan, the prophet, had predicted. David fasted and lay all night "upon the earth." He wept and prayed until the child died (2 Samuel 12:18).

The necessity for giving spiritual care to the child was clearly expressed by Christ in His post-Resurrection instruction to a broken-hearted Peter: "Feed my lambs" (John 21:15). That care should be of the kind so lovingly and sacrificially demonstrated by Hannah. She dedicated her child, Samuel, to lifetime service in the temple. "I prayed for the child . . . so now I give him to the Lord," she said. "For his whole life he will be given over to the Lord" (1 Samuel 1:27-28 NIV).

The strongest warning used by Jesus during His entire ministry was addressed to those who dared to harm a child. To rob a child of its innocence, to teach a child any evil was, He threatened, to risk a fate far, far worse than being fastened to a millstone and tossed into the sea. The pain felt by the patriarch, Job, centuries before, over the disadvantaged, damaged child was felt even more sharply by Jesus. "The fatherless child," mourned Job, "is snatched from the breast; the infant of the poor is seized for a debt" (24:9). Jesus insisted that such treatment must end.

Seeing our focus is on the *unmentioned*, we find ourselves wondering about the child called out from the crowd by Jesus to become an "object lesson." Jesus wanted to remind His disciples (and us!) that "child*like*ness" was an inescapable requirement for admission into the Kingdom of Heaven. Was it by accident that the boy was in the crowd that day? Was it out of childish curiosity that he pushed his way to the forefront? Did his parents know where he was, and, if so, were they pleased or displeased? And what was his name? Jesus may have known it, but He didn't mention it—at least not according to the accounts recorded by Mark (9:26) and Luke (9:47). In manhood, did that boy realize how close, when in the arms of Jesus, he had been to the Son of God?

The child may not have understood the lesson being taught, but surely the disciples, some of whom had been arguing about place and recognition, must have done so. Jesus wanted no misunderstanding about the kind of spiritual life that opens the gates of the Kingdom of Heaven. It was not that they should become as innocent as children. That would be impossible. The tainting experiences of adolescence and adulthood had already washed over their lives. In any event, He had "not come to call the righteous (the innocent), but sinners to repentance" (Matthew 9:13). He had come "to seek and to save that which was lost" (Luke 19:10). Nor was childlike simplicity, though beautiful and good, to be the condition of admission. The prerequisite was (and still is!) "except ye be *converted* and become as little children" (Matthew 18:3). Thereafter, the cultivation of such virtues as simplicity, artlessness and directness, should follow.

The child who responded to the invitation of Jesus, apparently without hesitation, did so trustingly. But more than a childish trust in Christ is necessary if one is to be among those who "enter into the Kingdom of Heaven." Nothing could illustrate trust more beautifully than the infant at its mother's breast. But that is *instinctual* trust. To enter the Kingdom of Heaven there must be a *conscious* and absolute dependency on God as Heavenly Father, on Christ as Saviour and Lord, and on the Holy Spirit as the unfailing Leader "into all truth." Then. . .

> *. . . Every virtue we possess*
> *. . . And every thought of holiness*
> *Are His alone!*
> Henriette Auber

CHAPTER 12

Stretcher-bearers Wanted!

In wartime pacifists and conscientious objectors have a rough passage. They are eulogized by those who admire their determination to live out their conviction not to kill or injure even the most ruthless enemies of their nation. They are lauded by people like Bertha Suttner, the Austrian novelist, whose powerful pacifist novel *Lay Down Your Arms* had immense social impact, and made her the first woman ever to be awarded the Nobel Prize (1905). By others they are damned. "The pacifist," said Theodore Roosevelt, during a speech given on July 27, 1917, "is as surely a traitor to his country and to humanity as is the most brutal wrongdoer." The statement was both uncharitable and untrue.

Conscientious objectors, with few exceptions, have loved their families and their country as passionately as any. They were ready to serve in the armed forces and do the most menial of work, but only as non-combatants. For the majority it was a matter of religious conviction (e.g., Quakers and many Salvationists); for others there were ethical reasons. But as corpsmen they served in the front lines. Their "weapons" were stretchers, medical equipment, mobile ambulances or the rendering of other auxiliary services. Armed with nothing but courage, stretcher-bearers were part of the most violent action. The battlefield was their acreage of selfless service. Their forays into no-man's land to rescue the wounded and the dying were often made under shot and shell. Personal danger was forgotten, and the stories of their heroism are legion. A Salvation Army officer, Henry ("Harry") John Andrews, MBE, a medical doctor serving with the forces, found himself "on duty" shortly after the end of the First World War, on the North-West Frontier of India. At the end of the Shinki Pass, near the Khajuri Post, there was an engagement with some of the fiercest tribesmen of the area. Andrews, ignoring his own danger, had only one thought—to collect the wounded, haul them to a van, dress their wounds quickly and send them off to safety. Just as he was about to step into the last van, he was killed. Posthumously, he was awarded the Victoria Cross, the most illustrious of all recognitions for bravery. All wars have had their Harry Andrews, all deserving of recognition. But in the main they remain unknown and unrecognized.

The foregoing is simply a preamble to the introduction of four stretcher-bearers whose compassion and resolution are noted, and deservedly so, by St. Mark in his Gospel (2:1-12). To this nameless quartet a very sick man owed both his physical cure and a brand-new spiritual life. According to the record the man was "sick of the palsy." That general term now has various, specific labels. Today, such an affliction would be more closely diagnosed, perhaps as Parkinson's Disease, Bell's Palsy, Muscular Dystrophy, or Cerebral Palsy, all debilitating, enfeebling ailments causing uncontrollable body movements or tremors. Today, the man would have the latest treatment in a modern clinic, access to effective drugs, and appropriate means of transportation. But, in the circumstances of the time, the sufferer and those around him had decided that a miracle was needed, that a total cure was the best of all worlds, better than treatment, better than therapy. And it could just be possible that the man called Jesus who had returned to "His own city," Capernaum (Matthew 9:1), might be the miracle-worker.

But what does one do when totally immobilized? Healing might be "there," but you are "here." The solution? Stretcher-bearers; men who would carry him on his pallet to the house, probably Peter's, where Jesus usually stayed, and where He was said to be preaching. But who were these helpers? Sons, nephews, neighbors? What did they do for a living? Could they get "time off"? Or were they professional transporters who would have to be paid? We assume that they were like all others in history's long tradition of stretcher-bearers—men of practical pity, willing to spend time and strength if a life could be saved. Details of personality and background are *unmentioned,* but that is not at all strange. Stretcher-bearers are not "limelighters". Very few receive the VC, though all may merit it; the reward lies in the satisfaction that comes from serving.

Arrived at their destination, the stretcher-bearers face a challenge. The crowd is so great that it is impossible to get in and reach the speaker. The courtyard is crowded with people who do not want to lose their place. The men carrying the litter cannot even reach the doorway. Is it to be an instance of "love's labor lost?" Or, if there is no apparent way, will they make one? The houses of the period had flat roofs, accessible by an outside stairway, and the stretcher-bearers decided that to lower the invalid through the roof was the only way in which he would ever get into the presence of Jesus.

The climb up the stairway would be awkward. Careful! Careful . . . ! Step by precarious step they reach the top. Though the roof was flat it was often used for such purposes as sleeping, drying vegetables, (Rahab [Joshua 2:6] used the roof to lay out her stalks of flax), ripening fruit, and for praying. But despite its varied use the roof was usually not made of very thick material, perhaps rough rafters with branches laid across, and the whole plastered with mud, so that to "take off the roof" and let someone down through it would be fairly easy, but damaging. It probably didn't take them long to "uncover the roof" and lower the patient. Nothing is said about property damages. Rather, the stretcher-bearers are commended by Jesus for their faith, and at this point their work ended. Their patient had been rescued. He was where he might be cured.

Today, when stretcher-bearers reach an ambulance or a field hospital, doctors and nurses take over. For the stretcher-bearer, however, it means a return to the battlefield in the hope of bringing another, and another, out of distress into comfort, out of anguish into relief.

The patient himself is no longer "sick of the palsy." He picks up his pallet, freed from illness and forgiven for his sins, and pushes his way out through the crowd. The anonymous stretcher-bearers climb back down the stairway and disappear. To be unidentified does not mean being useless! The world needs more, many more, stretcher-bearers. More of those whom Mother Teresa, out of her vast experience of human sin and suffering, calls *Carriers of Christ's Love.*

The Christian Stretcher-bearer's Song

Bring them in, bring them in,
Bring them in from the fields of sin.
Bring them in, bring them in,
Bring the wandering ones to Jesus!

Away on Business

Between Canada's two largest cities, Toronto and Montreal, there are 102 plane flights every day. That may not be a world record, but it indicates that a great many people are on the move, most of them, according to surveys, travelling on business. Many of them "do" business while they fly. There is a telephone within everyone's reach; communication has gone sky-high. From seven miles up, one can converse with a client or link with head office halfway round the earth. Lap-tops come into view as soon as the seatbelt sign goes off, and spreadsheets are gathering clusters of figures. As soon as the complimentary newspapers are distributed there is a synchronized rustling of pages until the financial section is reached. There is a collective sigh of relief when the headlines reveal that the Dow Jones Index is up. Eyes are scanning the columns for plus and percentage signs. It is commerce in the clouds.

When Jesus told the parable of the wedding banquet the king had prepared for his son (Matthew 22:1-14), He said that one of the absentees was a businessman. The king's servants reminded the man of the banquet (it was customary on the actual day of such an occasion for the guests to be reminded of the event and of the necessity for dressing themselves appropriately), but he ignored the message and went off "to his business" (v.5). Whatever his kind of business it was left *unmentioned*. But could any business have been more important than a royal banquet? (Such a red-carpet occasion in these days would imply a "command" attendance! Not to respond would be an act of unthinkable discourtesy and disgrace.) And had the man not read in the Scriptures about Daniel (8:27) who, centuries earlier, despite exhaustion and illness, "got up and went about the *king's* business"? But give this businessman his due. He may have ignored etiquette in not politely excusing himself, but he didn't descend to the ruffianism of other invitees. They actually mistreated the messengers and then killed them.

Perhaps the man's business really was urgent. Maybe his enterprise was teetering on the edge of bankruptcy and he was hurrying to a fateful meeting with his bankers. It certainly wasn't commerce in the clouds, but in biblical times there was plenty of commerce on earth, and, as today, trading was not without its burdens. For some it was "miserable business" (Ecclesiastes 4:8). For others it was exceedingly prosperous. A glance at the 27th chapter of Ezekiel, in which judgment is pronounced on Tyre, provides an informative window on the extensive trade of the times—metals, animals, fabrics, emollients, foodstuffs, gold, silver, gems, and much else. "The ships of Tarshish serve as carriers for your wares. You are filled with heavy cargo in the heart of the sea" (v.25).

What would we see if we could look into the mind and heart of the anonymous businessman whom Jesus used fictionally but illustratively in His parable? Selfishness? In any mad drive for profit, the pursuit of which eclipses all else, there is often a blood-red streak of avarice. In a letter written on the 15th of April, 1809, President Thomas Jefferson, of the United States of America, commented on "the selfish spirit of commerce, which knows no country, and feels no passion or principle, but that of gain." When personal gain is the only engine of the soul it is to be expected, as Louis B. Lundberg, U.S. banker and author bemoaned in his *Voices of Business*, "that all too often the businessman is thought of as having a cash register for a heart." It may ring often, but what is in the till at the end? "Is there something in trade," asks John Jay Chapman in his book, *Practical Agitation*, "that desiccates and flattens out, that turns men into dried leaves? Certainly there is. It is not due to trade, but to intensity of self-seeking."

Another hazard for the businessman is the temptation to ethical violation, to "get away" with something, to sell one's soul for "a mess of pottage"(Genesis 25:29-34). There are enough biblical biographies revealing manipulation and falsity leading to utter ruin to serve as clear warnings against untruth and deception. (Read Acts 5:1-5 and be introduced to Ananias and Sapphira.) Hopefully it was quoted out of context, but the London *Observer* of May 28, 1961, recorded some odious words of the then Soviet premier, Nikita

Krushchev: "When you are skinning your customers you should leave some skin on to grow again so that you can skin them again." This has rightly been described as "the brutalization of commercial ethics."

When Jesus included a businessman in His parable about the king's banquet it was not to imply that all businessmen were boorish or had lost their proper perspective on decency. Through the ages there have always been those who have demonstrated integrity in whatever business they followed. Rotary is perhaps the largest service club in the world. It is comprises men and women who represent an astonishing variety of occupations and professions. They are committed to what is called the Rotary 4-Way Test: 1. Is it the truth? 2. Is it fair to all concerned? 3. Will it build goodwill and better friendships? 4. Will it be beneficial to all concerned? If in every transaction the answer to these four questions is yes, then vocational excellence is assured. But the businessman of the parable would have failed the Four-Way Test. He wasn't interested in building good will. He was without respect for a king who, despite his regality, had extended a gracious invitation to the royal table. The man was lost in his own interests.

We should not probe so searchingly into the anonymity of the man of business and his *unmentioned* career that we miss the important, timeless teaching of the parable itself. The king's invitation was sincere. It was a repeated invitation, but there were those who were indifferent and discourteous. They thought they had better things to do than respond. Their disrespect rightfully earned the king's rejection. After all, the banquet did not depend upon *their* presence. Other guests would take their place—the poor, the maimed, the lame and the blind. And still others—the homeless, found under the hedges or huddled in shadowy corners. And still others—aimlessly wandering the lanes and byways. The king's palace would be full and the celebration would proceed. Everyone hearing Jesus tell the parable would sense the application. It was a reproof to the self-styled superiority of the Pharisees, to their exclusiveness and their worldliness. Places at the king's table would be occupied by the beggar and the friendless, the road-side laborer and the those wounded by life, all who are "weary and heavy-laden"—those who answered the king's call and responded to his invitation. The worldly heart—absorbed in the acquisition of riches, obsessed with the things of time and temporality—would risk the danger of missing that incomparable banquet in the Kingdom of Heaven, "the wedding supper of the Lamb" (Revelation 19:9). The point of the parable was certainly not left *unmentioned*. In its telling Jesus intended to reach the consciences of His hearers. "None of those men who were called," He said, "shall taste of my supper." To be invited is one thing; to accept the invitation is another. "For many be called, but few chosen" (Matthew 20:16). ". . . the rich man will fade away even while he goes about his business" (James 1:11), but "Blessed is he that shall eat bread in the kingdom of God" (Luke 14:15).

What's in the Bag?

"It's in the bag!" That's our elated exclamation when something we've hoped for, worked for, or negotiated is, or is about to be, possessed or realized. But why "the bag"? In its earliest history the bag was simply a useful receptacle, often made from the skin of an animal, with drawstrings at the mouth to close it and so protect the contents. Biblical references are numerous. In the book of Genesis (42:25) Joseph, now second-in-command only to Pharaoh himself, orders his brothers' bags to be filled with grain. In young David's shepherd's bag (1 Samuel 17:49) there is no grain, but five smooth stones. With one of them he will slay the Philistine giant, Goliath. In the 23rd year of the reign of Joash, King of Israel, money given to help in the repair of the Temple of the Lord was carefully put into bags by the royal secretary and the high priest (2 Kings.12:10). Through the princely prophet Isaiah (46:6 and following verses) God warns those who "pour out gold from their bags and weigh out silver on the scales" in order to make idols to which they will bow down and worship. He reminds any such idolaters that He is not to be counted equal to anyone or anything; "I am God, and there is no other" (Isaiah 46:9 NIV).

Three of the evangelists, Matthew, Mark and Luke, record in more or less the same words the instruction given by Jesus to the Twelve when He sent them out, two by two, to announce that "The Kingdom of Heaven is at hand." They were to go without the ordinary appurtenances of travel—no scrip (a pouch for carrying food), no money and no bag. In view of his later embezzling of the bag's contents, one wonders which of the Twelve was selected to be the travelling companion and co-worker of Judas? Would this *unmentioned* disciple have sensed even then that Judas was missing the point that one travels farther and more joyfully by faith than by funds?

Touchstone, the clown in Shakespeare's *As You Like It*, suggests: "Let us make an honorable retreat; though not with bag and baggage . . . " Thereafter, the phrase, "bag and baggage," jumps into common usage. The bag, of course, meant a purse. In his book, *Bible Sidelights from Shakespeare,* this writer's great-uncle, the Rev. William. Burgess, insists that "the greatest of the world's dramatists drew 'living water' from the inexhaustible wells of Scripture, and that he gathered his most precious pearls from its deepest depths." For Shakespeare, Judas Iscariot who "had the bag and bare what was put therein" (John 12:6) became the symbol of infamy. In five of his plays, *Richard II, Henry III, Richard III, Love's Labour Lost* and the one already mentioned, Shakespeare alludes to the traitorous character of Judas. But hardly in stronger terms than were used by the Apostle John to describe the weakness which led finally to Judas's act of betrayal. "He was a thief," says John, "as keeper of the money bag, he used to help himself to what was put into it" (John 12:6 NIV).

What *was* put into " the bag" is *unmentioned*. Was it much, or little? A Teacher and 12 men criss-crossing their homeland for three years would need some subsistence. They would have needed food, and some of it would surely have been bought. Several of the disciples had been fishermen, used to working hard in the outdoors, and probably had hearty appetites. One, who had been a tax-collector, may have been used to a richer lifestyle (he gave a great feast after deciding to throw in his lot with Jesus), but even with simpler nourishment, money would have been required to procure it.

And what about accommodation? Undoubtedly there would have been friends and relatives ready to offer traditional Eastern hospitality—friends like the family in Bethany with whom Jesus found rest and refreshment. But in three years there must have been occasions when rooms had to be rented. When Jesus said that "the Son of man hath not where to lay His head," (Matthew 8:20) He was admitting that He had no permanent abode. The foxes could retreat to their burrow. The birds had nests where they could harbor their young. He had no fixed address.

How much money there was "in the bag" at any one time is *unmentioned,* nor are we told from what various sources it originated. Most likely some came from the sale, by the disciples, of their possessions. Everything, apparently, was held in common, forecasting the time when, during the Apostolic ministry (Acts 4:32-35), those who had "lands or houses sold them, and brought the prices of the things that were sold, and laid them down at the apostles' feet." From time to time the funds were likely replenished by gifts from those who were grateful for the teachings of Jesus and for His healing ministry. Beneficiaries thus became benefactors; they "ministered unto Him of their substance" (Luke 8:3). Money contributed was also money given away. Unaware of the high drama of the moment, some of the disciples sharing in the Last Supper heard Jesus tell Judas to do quickly what he had to do. Because Judas was the treasurer they assumed he was being instructed to give some alms to the poor (John 13:29). One may gather from this that it was not unusual to assist the needy in this way.

It is beyond comprehension that someone who had been in the company of the Master for so long, who had listened time after time to His preaching and who had seen in Jesus the epitome of unsullied character, could have been a pilferer. Wasn't Judas present when Jesus warned against covetousness? "Provide yourselves bags which wax not old, a treasure in the heavens that faileth not, where no thief approacheth, neither moth corrupteth" (Luke 12:33). Judas had been entrusted with all the financial resources of the entire group, a responsibility given to him by Jesus Himself—a responsibility that should have led him to the further development of his capabilities but which, alas, led to his ruin. What a tragedy that Judas did not understand that "Money," as Thoreau put it, "is not required to buy one necessity of the soul."

It is sobering to think that the love of money could so grip a man that for what was really a paltry sum—nothing more than the price of a slave—Judas could actually betray his Master. In his privileged position Judas should have known what centuries later the celebrated Norwegian poet and dramatist, Henrik Ibsen, came to understand after his father's bankruptcy. From 15 years of age on, Ibsen had to fend for himself. "Money," he wrote, "may be the husk of many things, but not the kernel. It brings you food, but not appetite; medicine, but not health; acquaintances, but not friends; servants, but not loyalty; days of joy, but not peace or happiness."

The Apostle Paul said it even more succinctly: "The love of money is the root of all evil" (1 Tim. 6:10). It is a sad commentary on human nature that through the centuries since Paul gave this piece of advice to his "son in the Gospel," the love of money has for so many tragically superseded the love of integrity, honesty and accountability. The "hand in the bag" is still a widespread weakness. It is a despairing reality that in the world today so many are following in the footsteps of Judas. A dictator purloins a nation's treasury. A company director "feathers his nest" and brings down an international financial institution. A trusted employee raids the petty cash and sells *his* soul for "30 pieces of silver," or less. "There are men so incorrigibly lazy" wrote William Booth in *Darkest England And The Way Out*, "that no inducement you can offer will tempt them to work, so eaten up by vice that virtue is abhorrent to them, and so inveterately dishonest that theft is to them a master passion."

But Booth knew the remedy for such a master passion, and for all human sin—a passion for The Master! "Believe on the Lord Jesus Christ and thou shalt be saved" (Acts 16:31). For Judas that could have meant a glorious escape from lasting disgrace and a self-inflicted, horrid death.

The Cross-maker

Who was he, the man who made the cross on which Christ was crucified? Where did he live and work? Was he a Roman employed by the authorities to make nothing else but crosses? And did this particular carpenter know, we wonder, that he was making a cross for a fellow-carpenter, or that it was for the Son of God? Was it for him simply a matter of mass production, a totally impersonal job, since every now and again crosses were needed in great numbers and the sawdust on the floor of the carpenter's shop would be deep. The historian Josephus describes one mass crucifixion of no fewer than 2,000 Jews ordered by Quintilius Varus, a governor of Syria! Introduced by the Phoenicians and Persians, crucifixion was a form of punishment reserved by the Romans for foreigners or desperate criminals. And there were always criminals. Two were crucified with Jesus. That meant an order for three crosses.

The carpenter who made Christ's cross is *unmentioned,* so he remains nameless; but the name of the One nailed to it has echoed through all the centuries since. That Roman carpenter probably worked in a crowded shed on a back street in some insignificant hamlet. But the One for whom he made the cross accomplished on it the most significant of all acts—the procuring of salvation from sin and the hope of Heaven for all mankind

We speculate. Had this cross-maker ever heard of Jesus? If he had known that Jesus Himself had spent several years in a carpenter shop, would he have crafted this particular cross with extra care? Did it enter his mind that Jesus would have been familiar with all the tools of the trade—the adze, plummet, set-square, chisel, hammer? (A first-century tombstone bears the representation of a number of carpenter's tools, many of them basically the same as those used today—evidence that such tools are not easy to improve upon.)

Was it this unknown carpenter, or the authorities, who decided the shape of the three crosses to be provided? Were they to be of the common cross-beam shape, since part of the crucifixion procedure was to make the victim carry the cross-beam to the site of the final cruelty? Probably two other forms were sometimes ordered: the Capital-T shape that later became known as St. Anthony's cross; and the X-shaped cross, afterwards called St. Andrew's cross. The simple T-shaped cross was named for the Greek letter *TAU*, and is sometimes called the Old Testament cross because "Moses made a serpent of brass, and put it upon a pole" (Numbers 21:6-9). To look upon it meant healing from the savage bite of the snake. The "pole" was thought of as a cross because Jesus, in conversation with Nicodemus, likened His own death on the cross to the lifting up of the serpent in the wilderness by Moses (John 3:14). His being "lifted up," Jesus said, would "draw all men unto Him" and provide spiritual healing for the nations.

Some investigators have concluded that the making of crosses during the Roman occupation of Palestine required only the crudest kind of carpentry. The beams would be "knocked together," on the basis that the least refinement possible was most suited to the punitive purpose of the cross. "Rough and ready"—very rough!—was all that was required—a far cry from the crosses of smooth marble and costly gold that today commemorate the Crucifixion of Jesus. That comparison caused the eminent preacher, George F. Macleod, in *Only One Way Left*, to cry out with strong emotion: "I simply argue that the cross be raised again at the centre of the marketplace as well as on the steeple of the church. I am recovering the claim that Jesus was not crucified in a cathedral between two candles, but on a cross between two thieves; on the town garbage heap; at a crossroad so cosmopolitan that they had to write his title in Hebrew and in Latin and in Greek (or shall we say in English, in Bantu and in Afrikaans?); at the kind of place where cynics talk smut, and thieves curse, and soldiers gamble. Because that is where He died. And that is what He died about."

In view of this it doesn't really matter, does it, how roughly the cross is "knocked together?" It means that the commonest of woods will do. So, off to the wood-yard to pick up the necessary lumber, perhaps olive, perhaps sycamore—common, but solid. The finished cross must be strong enough to bear the weight of its quarry. Crosses made by the *unmentioned* carpenter were likely shorter than the lofty erections that artists and sculptors have since depicted. When the upright beam is dropped into the hole dug to receive it, and the cross-beam to which the victim has already been nailed or tied having been added, the condemned man will only be head and shoulders above the crowd.

So the cross is made and delivered. Jesus, already weakened by scourging, will shoulder its cross-beam as He staggers to that fatal place called Golgotha (in Latin, "Calvary" is the word for skull). When His strength fails, Simon of Cyrene will be dragooned by impatient soldiers to carry it the rest of the way. At Calvary, the cross serves its wretched purpose. The earthly life of the Son of Man comes to an end. But the Christ of the Cross will rise in Resurrection radiance. He will enter into His Father's glory and be mankind's eternal Saviour.

> *Behold! behold the Lamb of God*
> *On the cross;*
> *For us He sheds His precious blood*
> *On the cross.*
> *O hear His all-important cry,*
> *Why perish, blood-bought sinner, why?*
> *Draw near and see your Saviour die*
> *On the cross.*

Richard Jukes (1804-67)

Did the cross-maker, we wonder, ever come to know that Jesus not only died but rose again so that the *unmentioned* could one day, by His saving grace, be *mentioned* before His throne of glory?

CHAPTER 16

Peaceweavers

Two women mentioned in the New Testament are known only by their names and the fact that they could not agree with each other; surely not the most elevating of reasons for inclusion in a Book that continues to sell more than all others throughout the world. And what they disagreed about is *unmentioned.*

Members of the Christian church in Philippi obviously knew why these women, probably prominent in the life and work of the church, were at odds with each other. So did the Apostle Paul, because in his letter to the church (Philippians 4:2) he suggested that, as followers of Christ, Euodias and Syntyche should "be of the same mind." In other words, they should reconcile their differences and be at peace with each other. Their disagreement must have troubled, and perhaps surprised, Paul because, as he says, "They both worked hard for the Gospel" (v.3). He also suggested that they should be given every help in order to get the dispute settled. We are not told whether Paul's advice was heeded. We are left in the dark. We can only hope that the women eventually decided to "bury the hatchet," that they finally shook hands, or embraced, and perhaps with a "holy kiss" put their disagreements behind them.

Critics of the Church would squeeze every ounce of acid out of such a situation. How could two women calling themselves Christian and, indeed, having worked hard for the Gospel with such an eminent Christian personality as the Apostle Paul himself, possibly allow themselves to be estranged? The Church then, as now, would have benefited by having in the congregation some of those referred to in the Icelandic sagas as "peaceweavers." Their special duty and joy was to stitch together the ends of fraying friendships before a separation became suicidal. But let it be said at once, and emphatically, all disagreements are not necessarily of the devil, though the devil can certainly use them to further his own ends. Most families, even those of royal blood, experience moments of collision. In England's *Daily Mail* of October 19, 1989, Her Majesty Queen Elizabeth II was quoted as saying, "Like all the best families, we have our share of eccentricities, of impetuous and wayward youngsters, and of family disagreements." No parliament sits without debate and disagreement. And disagreement can be disagreeable. Listen to John Major, Prime Minister of the United Kingdom, at the centre of bitter dissension over Britain's membership in Europe. "I am walking," he said on October 28, 1992, "over hot coals suspended over a deep pit at the bottom of which are a large number of vipers baring their fangs."

Even saints can hold differing opinions and still be saintly. The very apostle who wanted the contention between Euodias and Syntyche to end was not without his own contentious episodes. When Peter and Barnabas shared the view that Jewish and Gentile Christians should eat their meals separately and not even celebrate the Lord's Supper together, it was Paul who objected. He felt that it would be a breach in the fellowship of the one body of Christ (Galatians 2:11-14). A conference was necessary to resolve the problem. On another occasion Paul was so upset by what he felt was the desertion of John Mark in the early stages of his first missionary journey, that he quarrelled sharply with Barnabas about John Mark's participation in the second great missionary venture. The solution— an agreement to disagree. Barnabas took John Mark as his companion. Paul took Silas, a Jerusalem Christian who had had a share in drawing up the official statement of the Apostolic Council (Acts 15:22), and who, like Paul, was a Roman citizen. It would be wrong to assume that these men had in any way lessened or lost their faith because of these controversies. Differences of opinion in no way diminished their dedication to the great Cause or their achievement in it.

We know what led to the disagreements Paul had with his brothers in the faith, and there is no mystery about them. But we haven't the slightest idea as to what provoked the friction between Euodias and Syntyche To know might have provided a salutary lesson for today's workers in the Church of Christ, ". . . as much as lieth in you, live peaceably with all men" (Romans 12:18). But let us be fair and list the worthy qualities of the two women. They were both active followers of Christ. Both were helpful to Paul in the work of the Gospel. Despite their differences they had not left the Christian community. They remained a vital part of the *ecclesia* in a city that badly needed the saving message of the Gospel.

Their church, the first in Europe, had been founded by the Apostle Paul himself during his second missionary journey (Acts 16), and the women would have been aware of its important history. They would also have known of that memorable meeting when Paul discovered a group of women at prayer beside the river, and when Lydia, whose business was the dyeing and selling of purple cloth, was baptized. Euodias and Syntyche may actually have been present. Both would also have known that the Philippian authorities had treated Paul and Silas badly during that pioneering visit. Paul had delivered a young girl of a "spirit of clairvoyance," and her owners, enraged at losing the income from her fortune-telling, had dragged Paul and Silas to the market square, and then on to face the magistrates. Sentenced, they were stripped, severely beaten and thrown into prison. But there had been a miraculous intervention; a mighty earthquake had rocked the jail and unchained them, and the terrified jailer was sure his prisoners would have escaped. Instead, they encouraged him to believe on the Lord Jesus Christ and be saved. As a result, the keeper of the prison and all his household were converted. Overjoyed at finding faith in God (v.34), the jailer took the prisoners into his own home, washed their wounds, and offered them food. A midnight baptismal service followed. The next morning the magistrates ordered the prisoners to be released.

All this would have been known to Euodias and Syntyche, perhaps at first-hand. They could hardly escape sensing that they were part of something remarkable, something permeated by Divinity—a fellowship of ordinary people like themselves, but one in which the very presence of God was manifesting itself. It was their city that had given birth centuries before to the warrior-emperor, Alexander the Great, but these women had come to know of One who was the greatest of all, and, despite disputation, they were still His followers.

The *unmentioned* cause of their "falling out" was not likely something of magnitude or great moment. If it had been, Paul would likely have mentioned it specifically and dealt with it sternly (1 Corinthians 5). Possibly it was something almost insignificant—a word out of place, perhaps. Christians are expected to be *"partners* in the Gospel" and not caustic combatants. Washington Irving, the American author who gave us the tale of Rip Van Winkle, observed that "A sharp tongue is the only edged tool that grows keener with use." Or was it a "putting down" by one of the other—so hurtfully embarrassing that it couldn't be overlooked? Or was it a trivial, uncharitable act, unexpected from a friend? But whatever the cause, and however minor, it had a painful outcome. Twenty centuries later it has not faded from the record. "How great a fire a little matter kindleth!" (James 3:5). On the 22nd of March, 1975, a technician checking for air leaks with a lighted candle caused a $100-million fire at the Brown's Ferry nuclear reactor in Decatur, Alabama. The fire burned out electrical controls, lowering the cooling water to dangerous levels. One lighted candle and a multi-million-dollar disaster! One fiery moment and a friendship explodes.

The story of Euodias and Syntyche should end with a great verse: "In the Name of Christ, as His true servants, Euodias and Syntyche were reconciled and their ministry in the church prospered." A cheering verse but, alas, it exists only in our imagination. We must hope that Paul's injunction (Phillippians 4:5) ". . . let your moderation be known . . ." was helpful, since, as Handley Moule in his commentary suggests, the deeper meaning of the phrase is "let your *yieldingness* be known unto all men." If the disagreement is apparent, so also should one's *yieldingness*—a willingness to give way, to be gracious, to be forgiving, to be Christlike, to be at peace one with another. Peace, after all, is a basic word in the Gospel message. It was the theme of the angels' Nativity song in the skies over Bethlehem. It was Christ's final legacy, His last gift to humanity: "My peace I leave with you . . . "

If we knew the end of the story it may be that Euodias and Syntyche became as harmonious in their relationship as that other duo to whom Paul, when writing to the Christians in Rome, asked to be remembered—Tryphena and Tryphona, possibly sisters, who "work so hard in the Lord" (Romans 16:12 NIV)—and, apparently, *without* disagreement! Perhaps they were "peaceweavers."

Storm Centre

Nero is a name written in blood on the pages of Roman history. In the New Testament he is the "Caesar" related to Paul's trial (Acts 25-28), and it is "Nero's household" that sends greetings via the Apostle Paul to the Christians in Philippi (Philippians 4:22). Members of that "household"—*unmentioned* in gender, age, personality, status and heroism—claim our interest. But-in order to appreciate their steadfast devotion to Christ and their uncompromising loyalty to the nascent Christian Church, at whatever cost, one must try to sense the temper of the times during the capricious and vile reign of the Imperator Nero Claudius Caesar Augustus Germanicus.

If an evil nature can be inherited, Nero had the misfortune to be the son of Gnaeus Domitious who, according to Will Durant's *History of Civilization [Caesar and Christ]*, "enhanced the libidinous reputation of his family by adultery, incest, brutality, and treason." Nero's mother, Agrippina II, who had married at the age of 13, was determined to shape her son's career, and from the moment he ascended the throne at the age of 17, the reign became a matriarchate. Nero's father, knowing his wife's ancestry and his own, concluded "no good man can possibly be born from us." When Nero sought to rid himself of his mother's domination, she reacted by trying to unseat him and put Britannicus, his step-brother, in his place. Nero aborted the plot by having Britannicus poisoned and his mother put into reclusive isolation until she, too, was murdered. He divorced and murdered his first wife, and reputedly kicked his second wife to death. He was at the centre of scandal after scandal, and at 25 years of age was described as "a degenerate with swollen paunch, weak and slender limbs, fat face, blotched skin, curly yellow hair, and dull grey eyes."

In AD 64 fire broke out in the Circus Maximus. It burned for nine days, rampaging through the city. When it died out, two-thirds of Rome lay in ruins and ash. Did Nero, as the saying has it, "fiddle while Rome burned"? More accurately, the records show that he watched the conflagration from the tower of Maecenas while irrationally singing and accompanying himself on the lyre, fancying himself as singer, musician and actor. Hundreds of thousands of citizens roamed the streets, homeless and hungry, while rumors multiplied that Nero himself had ordered the fire so that Rome could be rebuilt to match his own fantasies. To quash the allegations Nero had to find a scapegoat. Actually, he found many.

For enlightenment we turn to the writings of the Roman senator Tacitus, perhaps the greatest of the republic's historians. He describes the city of Rome under Nero as a "common sink into which everything infamous and abominable flows like a torrent." In such a coarse milieu it was not difficult for Nero to find profligate wretches who were willing to testify that the real incendiaries belonged to a rapidly-growing sect whose members gave allegiance to a Jewish teacher named Jesus whom they regarded as the Messiah. They were called Christians. A number of them were quickly convicted, and, in the words of Tacitus, "were put to death with exquisite cruelty, and to their sufferings Nero added mockery and derision. Some were covered with skins of wild beasts and left to be devoured by dogs; others were nailed to crosses; numbers of them were burned alive; many, covered with inflammable matter, were set on fire to serve as torches during the night. . . . At length the brutality of these measures filled every breast with pity. Humanity relented in favor of the Christians."

For some it was too late. The "scapegoats" had been found and had been tortured. Scapegoats—dying for love of the One who was Himself the Divine Scapegoat for mankind's sins! In reality, Nero's scapegoats were towering heroes and heroines of the faith who felt themselves linked in love to their brothers and sisters in Christ in distant Philippi. So much is compacted into a single sentence: "All the saints send you greetings, *especially those who belong to Caesar's household.*" It is uncertain whether Paul meant "saints" (believers) who actually served the emperor in one or other of his palaces, or those who were part of the civil service which naturally operated under the emperor's domination. Among them, some freedmen, some slaves, accountants, administrators, secretaries, servants, and others performing humbler duties. Whatever their station in Nero's "household," they belonged first of all to "the household of Jesus Christ."

At the time of writing to the Philippians Paul himself was a prisoner in Rome. Eventually, he and the Apostle Peter would both meet death under Nero's edict. It is a challenging reminder that it is gloriously possible to live the Christian life where tyranny, immorality and genocide appear to have the upper hand. William Booth, Founder of The Salvation Army, once said that if a water-lily could bloom in pristine whiteness in a slimy, muddy pond, then so could a man or woman, by the grace of God, live a life of purity in the midst of impurity. Could he have been thinking about "those of the household of Caesar?"

While the storm of persecution and oppression swirled destructively across the whole Roman republic, the Christian witness not only survived, but triumphed. As Tacitus remarked, the sympathy of the population eventually was with the Christians. In contrast, Nero's omnipotence ruined him and he came to a tragic end. He tried to poison himself, but failed out of fear. He tried to drown himself in the Tiber but courage was lacking. About to be arrested he thrust a dagger into his throat, then faltered. His freedman helped him to press the blade home. He was 31 years of age.

The Roman Empire is no more, but the heroism, the ready martyrdom of those Christians who were "of the household of Caesar" lives on. They are among those eulogized in the 11th Chapter of Hebrews: "They were stoned, they were sawn asunder, were tempted, were slain with the sword . . . being destitute, afflicted, tormented; (of whom the world was not worthy)." Their witness was not in vain. Sown in blood, the seed of Christianity took strong root. The day would come when, with Nero forgotten, the Emperor Constantine, despite wars and politics, would become the great espouser of Christianity. He told Eusebius that he had seen a flaming cross in the sky, with the words, "In this sign thou shalt conquer," and conquer he did. He dreamed in an Old Testament kind of revelation that a voice commanded him to have his soldiers mark upon their shields the letter X with a line drawn through it and curled around the top—the symbol of Christ. His troops moved into battle behind a standard carrying the initials of Christ interwoven with a cross, and as victors became the welcomed and unchallenged masters of the West.

"The saints of Nero's household" summon today's pilgrims on the Christian path to "endure to the end," whatever the perils of the way and its ultimate cost. Where Paul, according to tradition, was beheaded there stands today a Christian church. Its spire bears a cross, not the Roman eagle! Unbelievably, some modern hymnaries have dropped the following lines, but they remain demonstrably and incontrovertibly true:

> *Crowns and thrones may perish,*
> *Kingdoms rise and wane,*
> *But the Church of Jesus*
> *Constant will remain.*
> *Gates of Hell will never*
> *'Gainst the Church prevail;*
> *We have Christ's own promise,*
> *And that cannot fail.*

Sabine Baring-Gould

The Royalty of Wisdom

Artist's conceptions of them appear on millions of Christmas cards. They are staged in pomp and splendor in every Nativity play, and in most carolfests three regally-arrayed males sing words and music provided by J. H. Hopkins: "We three kings of Orient are, bearing gifts we traverse afar." With rollicking rhythm and often with theatrical verve the vocalists remind us of the visit paid by those "wise men from the east" who, following a special star, reached Bethlehem in time to worship the newborn Christ-child (Matthew 2:1-12).

But who were these "wise men"? Were they actually monarchs? Where did they come from? From "the east," the record says. But what does that mean? From what kingdom? What city? The record concludes by saying that they "returned to their own country." But to which country? What was their nationality? There is no denying the importance of their visit; it shines through the story—their courage in the presence of Herod the Great, whose life of splendid misery had left him half-maddened, and their total reverence in the presence of an Infant King discovered in the humblest of resting-places. But for the most part the details are *unmentioned*.

Oriental tradition, supported by such worthy fathers of the Church as St. Augustine and St. Chrystostom, maintained that there were 12 who followed "His star." The more commonly-held belief has been that there were just three, based on mention of the gifts they brought—gold, frankincense and myrrh. Matthew speaks of "wise men" in the plural, but mentions no actual number. The Venerable Bede, known as "the father of English Church history" and greatly respected for his meticulous separating of historical fact from hearsay and tradition, concluded that the "wise men" numbered three. He actually named and described them, and suggested that they were, respectively, descendants of Shem, Ham and Japheth, the three sons born to Noah in his 500th year. Melchior, Bede asserted, was an old man with white hair and a long beard. Caspar was ruddy in appearance, a beardless youth. Balthasar was swarthy and in the prime of life. Thus, according to Bede, youth, middle-age and old-age knelt in homage at the feet of the Infant Christ—an appealing thought.

Matthew's simple statement, "there came wise men from the east" (v.1), however, leaves unanswered any questions about their origins and their status. How did the idea that they were "kings" arise? Was it because Isaiah, the princely prophet, had predicted that "Gentiles shall come to thy light, and kings to the brightness of thy rising" (Isaiah 60:3)? Was it because, as non-Jews, the "wise men" came asking "Where is He that is born King of the Jews?" (v.2). If they *were* kings in their own right it is not surprising that they would first of all, on arrival in Jerusalem, go to the glittering palace of King Herod, and not to a lesser source, to ask for directions to the object of their search.

Their visit, however, seems to bespeak the royalty of wisdom far more than the grandeur of a throne. Coming, as they did, from the East, their journey could have originated in Media, noted for its sages and its astrologers. The historian Herodotus tells us that in that part of the world there was a priestly class which devoted itself solely to the study of celestial phenomena in relationship to human affairs. The "East" could also have meant Mesopotamia where there had been scholars since the time of Nebuchadnezzar specializing in the knowledge of Palestinian concerns. Kings they may have been, but "wise men" they were without a doubt. Wise because, at whatever cost, they made the trek to Bethlehem; they found the Christ-child and worshipped Him; and they presented their costly gifts, each with its own significance. Wisely, they then defied an imperial instruction to return to Herod by journeying home by another way. Their coming from the Gentile world brought Gospel history into accord with Jewish belief. This was the fruit of their wisdom.

Kings? Or wise men? Or both? There is no objective history to help us decide. If it were to be a choice between kingship and wisdom, let wisdom be exalted. Monarchy may be the oldest form of government, and most early peoples knew no other system. But kings have come and gone, and absolute monarchies have disappeared. Lord Byron, the English poet, wrote a prophetic entry into his journal for January 13, 1821. "The king-times are fast finishing. There will be blood shed like water, and tears like mist; but the peoples will conquer in the end. I shall not live to see it, but I foresee it." In contrast, wisdom occupies an enduring throne. "Raphael paints wisdom. Handel sings it. Phidias carves it. Shakespeare writes it. Wren builds it. Columbus sails it. Luther preaches it," declares philosopher Ralph Waldo Emerson in *Society and Solitude.* But it took one who was a king himself to point the way to the acquisition of true wisdom: "The fear of the Lord is the beginning of wisdom" (Psalm 111:10).

"There came wise men from the east . . ."

And Now, a Hymn

The last collective act of Jesus and His disciples following their final meal together was to sing a hymn (Matthew 26:30; Mark 14:26). They then stepped out into the midnight silence, and quietly made their way to the Garden of the Oil Press, which is called Gethsemane, on the western slopes of the Mount of Olives. The fateful shadow of the cross had already fallen across the group, and the singing would surely have been tremulous, even though the disciples at this moment had no full comprehension of the horror that was soon to engulf them. Two thousand years later Christian congregations cannot sing Hassler's *Passion Chorale*, "O sacred head now wounded . . ." without being moved close to tears.

The hymn used by Jesus and the 11 disciples is *unmentioned* in the Scriptural record, though hymns were common among the ancient Hebrews, and evidence of their popularity appears in the Bible. In the Book of Psalms the Israelites had a ready-made hymnary, and they sang from it during all the great religious celebrations such as Passover, the Feast of the Tabernacles and Pentecost. One section, known as the Hallel (the Hebrew word for "Praise") which included Psalms 113 to 118, was often used. If this were the choice on this particular occasion which was so full of sadness and foreboding, one can imagine the deep emotion with which were sung such words as, *"The sorrows of death compassed me, and the pains of hell gat hold upon me; I found trouble and sorrow"* (Psalm 116:3). Or again, *"What shall I render unto the Lord for all His benefits toward me? I will take the cup of salvation, and call upon the name of the Lord"* (Psalm 116:12, 13). Or yet again, *"The Lord is my strength and song, and is become my salvation"* (Psalm 118:14). *"The stone which the builders refused is become the head stone of the corner. This is the Lord's doing; it is marvellous in our eyes"* (Psalm 118:22, 23).

Hymns are to be found in the literature of nearly every

religion, but so far as we are able to judge, save in the Hebrew and Christian, they have rarely been used as a constant and integral part of worship. No form of worship requiring song was instituted by Moses. No order of singers is included among the officers of the tabernacle. The Old Testament, however, abounds with references to songs— spontaneous, improvised songs that celebrated a divine intervention in the affairs of a nation or the life of an individual. Examples are the praiseful songs of Moses and Miriam addressed to Jehovah for His deliverance of the Israelites from Egypt (Exodus15:1-18). Eventually, sacred song found its way into the regular services of the Temple, and the Book of Psalms became the liturgical hymn-book of the Jewish Church. The Levites used to sing a different Psalm in the Temple on each day of the week, sometimes so loudly, recorded one rabbinical scholar, that the sound could be heard as far as Jericho, a distance of about 12 miles! It is obvious that the Book of Psalms, which has no equivalent in the New Testament, so sounded the deepest notes of the soul in joy and sorrow, in darkness and light, that it was not for one era only, but for all time.

Singing undoubtedly formed a part of both the social and public worship of the apostolic age. The disciples, dismissed by the rulers in Jerusalem, gathered together and, with one accord, lifted up their voices in a song that was partly the inspiration of the moment and partly from the Book of Psalms. In the Philippian dungeon, Paul and Silas prayed and sang praises to God, and Paul exhorted both the Ephesians and Colossians to use Psalms, hymns and spiritual songs. Secular historians noted that Christians expressed their faith in song quite naturally. Pliny wrote to the Emperor Trajan in AD 110 that "they (the Christians) sang in alternate verses a hymn to Christ." Psalm 133, according to Tertullian, was sung at the Christian *agapai* (love-feasts). It has been well said that "the Church has been singing the Psalms ever since, and she will go on singing them until she takes up the new song in the heavenly city" (Revelation 5:9).

It is to Martin Luther that credit belongs for making the Latin hymns he knew so well attractive to a larger public. He did this by wedding the words to secular and sacred tunes that were the favorites of the people. He began a movement that swept across Germany, France and England, inspiring noted composers to set the Psalms to music. This "bridge period" merits study far beyond the intention and ability of this brief commentary.

Isaac Watts, while not the first writer of hymns in English, is considered to be the real founder of English hymnody. In our hymn-singing age it is difficult, especially for younger people, to realize the strength and even violence of the prejudice that existed against the introduction of hymns into church worship. Watts himself, as a 15-year-old youth, found the use of the metrical Psalms tedious and, one Sunday morning, returning from what he considered to be "a particularly atrocious service" complained to his father. The father told him to "try and mend the matter." Isaac did so before the evening service, and had such success with his first attempt, *Behold the glories of the Lamb,* that he was asked to compose more hymns. Eventually, there were sufficient to make up a volume. Isaac was a precocious child. He was taught Latin when four years of age, Greek when he was eight or nine, French when he was 11, and Hebrew when he was 12. But unhappily, the physical appearance of the illustrious Dr. Isaac Watts (1674-1748) did not match the quality of his mind. He was only five feet in height. He had a hooked nose, small, piercing eyes, a frail and sickly body. A beautiful and accomplished young lady, says Albert Edward Bailey in his book, *The Gospel in Hymns,* fell in love with Watts through his poetry, having never seen him. When the two met her disillusionment was instantaneous, while he fell deeply in love with her. She refused his proposal of marriage in plain, honest language: "Mr. Watts," she said, "I only wish I could admire the casket as much as I admire the jewel." Watts never married, but he and the lady remained lifelong friends.

The appearance of Watts' hymns was the spark that kindled a noble fire that still burns in our time. In honored succession we find the names of Philip Doddridge, Joseph Addison, Joseph Grigg, who are among those who brought the Psalter into the vernacular. Then came John and Charles Wesley with their hymns of personal experience. In the 50 years preceding the rise of the Wesleys and George Whitefield, England had reached its lowest pitch of moral degradation. Even psalm-singing had fallen into its worst estate. John Wesley at once began to translate some of the German hymns, and methodically introduce them. Once translated, he would try out the hymn in an early morning devotional service. He used what we have come to call, "lining out a song." Because music was not available, and because some of the congregation could not read even if the words were accessible, the leader would sing one line which the congregation would then repeat. And so on, throughout the hymn. Wesley would then sing it at weeknight services and, finally, introduce it formally in the larger Sunday gatherings. In 1737 he published his *Collection of Psalms and Hymns*—the first hymnal ever used in an Anglican Church. It included no fewer than 70 selections from Isaac Watts. John's brother, Charles, was the 18th child of his parents. His conversion released a flood of hymns, 6,500 of them, built on hundreds of Scripture texts and dealing with every conceivable aspect of Christian experience.

The floodgates of hymn-writing burst open across the world. An entire library of books would be required to provide the history of the tidal outpourings of prayer and praise of which all Christians today are the fortunate beneficiaries. Who could be in Wales without hearing William Williams' *Guide Me, O Thou Great Jehovah*? Or in the deep south of the United States without singing John Newton's *Amazing Grace*, and seeking to know the astonishing life-story of its writer—slave-trader turned cleric? Hymn-singing is now global. There are nationally-produced hymnaries embracing many languages. In them, ancient hymns are side by side with those written to express the religious fervor of our contemporary world. They are treasures to be preserved. Many songs and choruses used today in worship services will, however, have a brief life. They lack melody, some abysmally so; they lack also the doctrinal strength with which the great hymns are permeated, and in which the poets invested their intimate knowledge of the Scriptures, their informed theology, their scholarship and their religious ardor. A hymn, someone has suggested, is "a doctrinal statement in verse that must be sung."

"And when they had sung a hymn they went out . . ."

No Fish in the Ark

In the biblical record of the great deluge and the Ark which carried Noah and his wife, together with their three sons and their wives, to safety (Genesis 6), other passengers were "every beast after his kind, and all the cattle after their kind, and every creeping thing that creepeth upon the earth after his kind, and every fowl after his kind, every bird of every sort" (Genesis 7:14). The only animals not inventoried for preservation in the Ark were the cold-blooded aquatic animals we call fish. While the deluge meant death for all "that moved *upon the earth*"—mankind and animals—for that part of God's creation that lived in the waters it simply meant an increased habitat! If there was a reason in the Divine Mind for differentiating between "land" animals and "aquatic" animals, it is *unmentioned*.

What *is* mentioned is that an all- holy God "saw that the wickedness of man was great in the earth," and "repented the Lord that He had made man . . . and it grieved Him at His heart" (Genesis 6:6). He then decided to cleanse the earth of its vileness and to begin again. Evil was to be "washed away." Noah, however, was to be spared. He had "found grace in the eyes of the Lord" (Genesis 6:8) as a man who lived by faith in a corrupt generation, a righteous man who wanted to do God's will (see Hebrews 11:7) in a world ruined by wickedness. He had stood alone, bravely, exercising true faith in God. And now God wanted him to be the *alpha* of a new humanity. "God blessed Noah and his sons" (Genesis 9:1), and assured them that never again would He "smite every living thing." Instead, He gave them (and us!) a gracious, bedrock promise on which the confidence of mankind could securely rest: "While the earth remaineth, seedtime and harvest, and cold and heat, and summer and winter, and day and night shall not cease" (Genesis 8:22).

So there were no fish in the ark. There was no necessity for Noah to equip one of the three storeys of his craft with aquariums for their care and perpetuation. It would have been an unthinkable task. According to the ichthyologists (scientists who specialize in that branch of zoology that has to do with fish), there are more than 20,000 species inhabiting the oceans and the seas of our planet, more than all other species—birds, reptiles, mammals and amphibians—combined. They glide through the deeps in a marvellous variety of size, shape and color. In size they range from the pygmy goby of the Philippines which, at its longest, reaches half an inch, to the whale shark which grows to 60 feet in length and weighs more than 20 tons. In shape there is an amazing variation. While most are "torpedo-shaped," some are flattened and rounded, as in flounders, and others are vertical and angular, as in sea horses. In coloration they rival the 256 color-spectrum of a modern computer screen, and possibly more vividly. Wherever there is water, whatever the altitude or depth, there are fish. They are found three miles high in the Andes mountains in Lake Titicata, and six miles below the surface of the Pacific Ocean. About 60 percent of fish species live in marine waters near coasts where there is an abundance of food. The remaining 40 percent are found in fresh waters such as the Great Lakes, which are shared by Canada and the United States.

The incredible diversity in the fish family reflects God's desire in creation to provide a variety of wonders for the interest and appreciation of mankind. The most colorful of all fish is the appropriately-named angelfish. Some are classified as majestic angelfish; others as emperor angelfish. Their exotic colors serve to warn off intruders. Other species have great strength. The chinook, or king salmon, native to northern Pacific coasts from Japan to California, undertake the longest spawning migrations of all, some to nearly 2,500 miles! There are also oddities in the sea. The archerfish ejects jets of water from its gill chambers and shoots them at insects. The freshwater four-eyed fish, found in Central America and parts of South America, has eyes that divide at the water line. It can see above and below the surface of the water at the same time. In contrast, the brill has both eyes located on one side of the head. The lower, colorless side is blind. South Africa has its clingfish, so named because of the powerful hold it can take on rocks with a large sucking disc on the underside of its forebody. The electric eel can produce a field of more than 600 volts, intense enough to kill small animals and stun large animals or humans. There are fish, like the gurnard, that "walk" slowly along the ocean floor, while a typical flying fish glides in flights above the ocean's surface.

From earliest times the sea has provided a generous harvest of food for humans, though sadly today's food basket of the sea is threatened by overfishing and pollution of the world's waters. The existence of a number of species is jeopardized and, as well, the nourishment for an ever-increasing human population. Even today there are relatively primitive societies that depend almost wholly on fish for food. In many industrialized nations fish still constitutes a major part of the diet. It is said that the search for codfish led French fishermen to the discovery of Canada, and that villages sprang up on the coast of Norway, Scotland, Japan, and other countries wherever shoals of herring regularly came close to shore.

In New Testament times there was a regular industry on the shores of the Sea of Galilee for salting-down fish and packing them into barrels, and the products were sold not only in Palestine but as far west as Rome. A. C. Bouquet, in his book *Everyday Life in New Testament Times*, records that the pious fishermen of Tiberias once entered into an agreement not to fish on *any* of the days of the feasts of Passover and Tabernacles, instead of on some of them. The result was a serious shortage of fresh fish, never very plentiful inland at the best of times, so that the public had to fall back on salt fish, or go without altogether. It was from such a group of Galilean fishermen that Jesus called a number of His disciples. Though He was a carpenter and they were the experts when it came to fishing, twice Jesus gave them instructions about making a good catch—once when calling them to be "fishers of men," and later, after His Resurrection. In both instances He told them precisely where and how the fish were to be caught, even though they had "toiled all night and caught nothing" (Luke 5:5; John 21:5). It was common custom during the time of Jesus for people making a journey to carry with them some bread and salt fish—the wayside lunch of the times. Possibly the "two fishes" which, in the hands of Jesus, were multiplied to feed the 5,000 (Matthew 14:17), or the "few little fishes" that were multiplied to meet the hunger of the 4,000 (Matthew 15:35), had been salted to preserve their edibility.

No fish in the Ark. But the Deluge, meant to rid the earth of unholiness, was evidently not long-lasting in its effect. Centuries later, the prophet Hosea, and similarly the prophet Zephaniah, found it necessary to warn the children of Israel that God would inevitably sit in judgment against their sin, and that the consequences would be serious: "Therefore shall the land mourn, and everyone that dwelleth therein shall languish, with the beasts of the fields, and with the fowls of heaven; *yea, the fishes of the sea also shall be taken away*" (Hosea 4:3; see also Zephaniah 1:3).

Silence to Sound

Did the Apostle John know that curiosity might sometimes get the better of us? So many highlights in the life of Jesus, particularly during the period of His ministry, are recorded telegraphically—a story in a sentence, a parable in a paragraph. Perhaps that is why John finished his Gospel by saying ". . . there are also many other things which Jesus did, the which, if they should be written every one, I suppose that even the world itself could not contain the books that should be written." He emphasizes the conclusion to which he has come with a resounding, Amen!

If, for instance, a biographer had all the facts, what could he not do with the life of the man from Decapolis who was "deaf, and had an impediment in his speech" (Mark 7:32), and who was healed by Jesus (Mark 7:32-35)? There would be a vivid description of what the man's life was like before the healing. And afterwards. Several chapters could be devoted to the unusual, progressive method of healing used by Jesus. We, as today's readers of the New Testament, have only the short version of the miracle given us by the Apostle Mark. Brief as it is, questions begin to surface. "Why did Jesus first look heavenward? Was that upward look, a glance towards God, an acknowledgment that every supernatural act is dependent upon God the Father's eternal omnipotence? "He sighed," Mark next tells us. But was that so unusual? When there are special pressures upon the mind and heart, isn't a sigh a natural, human reaction? That sigh, surely, must have been a wordless exclamation from the very heart of Christ. Sin had spoiled the Creator's plan. The man standing before Him represented the many whose bodies were burdened with disease or deformity. The perfection of Eden had long since degenerated into global imperfection. And He was to be the Saviour. Little wonder He sighed. What He was about to do for the disadvantaged man He wanted to do for all mankind—open all ears so that the Good News of Salvation might be heard, and unfasten every tongue so it might offer praise and glory to the Sovereign Lord.

Then Jesus spoke the miraculous, liberating word, "*Ephphatha*" ("Be opened!"). Not only were the man's ears opened, but "his tongue was loosed." Marvellous! Incredible! Now, the man could not only hear, but speak. In fact, Mark tells us, "he spake plainly" (v.35). But what did the man *say*? Disappointingly, what he said is *unmentioned*. Undoubtedly he expressed his gratitude. Perhaps he shouted his thanks at the top of his new-found voice

For the first time the man hears himself speaking. But there are other sounds as well. He hears the ejaculations of the onlookers who couldn't wait to spread the news of the miracle. He hears Jesus telling the crowd—not once, but twice—that they should keep their own counsel. Probably he heard much else—the clip-clop of passing horses, the buzz of a fly circling his face, the sharp snort of a plodding camel, the hilarity of children at play, nearby traders hawking their wares—for the first time ever he hears the cacophony of life and humanity.

Until now the man has been imprisoned in silence. To him sound is wonderful. He has escaped from a silence that most of the *un*deaf occasionally feel they cannot live without. Most of us who have been spared deafness appreciate a little silence. Now and again we want to hear ourselves think. We want to hear what lies behind the clamor of the world. We want to leave words at the door, as the Japanese leave their shoes, when we enter a silent sanctuary. Silence elevates us. The highest honor we can pay a performer whose artistry has led us into a higher realm is not applause, but absolute silence. Searching for silence people climb mountains, tramp along deserted shores, work in soundproof studios. Discovering silence they can then not only think their own deeper thoughts, but can hear someone else think. "God cannot be found in noise and restlessness," says Mother Teresa in her book, *A Gift for God*. "See how nature—trees, flowers, grass—grows in silence; see the stars, the moon and the sun, how they move in silence. We need silence to be able to touch souls."

Tell this to the congenitally deaf and they can't understand. To *search* for silence in order to find inner peace and tranquillity, as do the Trappist monks, is one thing. But to be permanently incarcerated in silence—not hearing any spoken words, denied the rapture of great music, unalarmed by the danger-screech of tires—is something else. It is like being locked in a cell of soundlessness, with little hope of parole.

We have infinite sympathy for the deaf and admire the way in which so many of them overcome the handicap, despite frustration. The gigantic genius of Ludwig van Beethoven could not be thwarted by deafness, though he did not by any means accept it passively. He knew despair and resignation, but also defiance. When he realized that his deafness was incurable he wrote this prayer: "O God give me strength to be victorious over myself, for nothing may chain me to this life. O guide my spirit, O raise me from these dark depths, that my soul, transported through Thy wisdom, may fearlessly struggle upward in fiery flight. For Thou alone understandest and canst inspire me." It was said of Beethoven that "deafness hushed the noises of the material world that he might better hear the whisperings of the spirit pervading it." Out of his silent world came a torrent of unsurpassed composition, including his magnificent *Ninth Symphony* in which a choral *finale* enhances the triumphal accents of the orchestral climax. Using the words from Schiller's *Hymn to Joy,* Beethoven, out of his soundless universe, gave today's church congregations throughout the world the sounds on which could also float Henry van Dyke's stirring paean of praise: *Joyful, joyful, we adore Thee, God of glory, Lord of love.*

Cured by Jesus, that deaf man, centuries before Beethoven, regained what the master musician had lost. But there was no relief at hand for Beethoven, and years would pass before the sciences of sign language and lip reading would be established and available. In 1760 the Abbé Michel de l'Epée had the genius to take the self-invented methods of communication of the Parisian deaf community and put them together to form a primitive kind of sign language. Almost simultaneously a German, Samuel Heinicke, began to teach lip reading. But for almost a century there was confusion as to which was the better system. Nevertheless, concern about the education of the deaf and mute increased steadily. In the Western world the first permanent, and free, school for the deaf was opened in 1817 in Hartford, Connecticut. It was one more "work of mercy" to be added to the many that through the ages had flowed out of the Church and its ministry. An Episcopalian clergyman by the name of Thomas

Hopkins Gallaudet was the instigator. Today's North American deaf students know the name well. To attend the Gallaudet College in Washington, D.C., with its rich tradition and its superb academic standard, is to grasp the golden grail of education.

To the hapless man standing before Jesus on the eastern shore of the Sea of Galilee the names of L'Epée, Heinicke and Gallaudet would mean nothing. For him, the name of Jesus means everything. Because of Jesus he is no longer deaf, he is no longer voiceless. Now he hears. Now he speaks. *Ephpha-tha* has done it. His liberation is from God, by the Son of God!

Paying the Price

The man inside might know the difference, but looking from the outside at a display of pearls in the shop window, we simply can't tell one from another. On Honolulu's main street, store after store confidently advertises, "Genuine Oyster Pearls." But what is meant by "genuine?" Is it a genuine saltwater pearl, or is it a genuine freshwater pearl? Or perhaps it is only a genuine "cultured" pearl. We wonder if the pearl that catches our eye is genuinely genuine, the result of that slow, mysterious, nacreous process of Nature itself a pearl that can't be man-made, only copied?

The Romans who occupied Judea during the period of Jesus' earthly ministry, unlike the Spartans and Stoics who were committed to austerity and restraint, were exceedingly fond of jewelry. Their women considered gems an important part of their adornment. They favored rings, necklaces, amulets, and brooches made of gold. Typical of the reckless extravagances of her time, Lollia Paulina, the ex-wife of the ill-fated Emperor Caligula, once wore a dress covered from head to foot with emeralds and pearls. We smile at her idea of *haute couture,* but smile even more when history tells us that she always carried with her the receipts to show what her jewelry had cost. Generally speaking, the more massive, the more glittering the jewelry, the more it was coveted. Elegance was frequently reduced to gaudy flamboyance. But when elegance was required, when a special occasion demanded refinement, ropes of pearls, exquisite in their color and arrangement, were worn with pride. It was not unknown for an aristocratic Roman to wear his entire fortune, in the form of rings or other ornaments, on his person As a patrician, he could not bear to be parted from his wealth.

The parable that Jesus told about the pearl merchant and the pearl of supreme perfection (Matthew 13:45-46) had a significance that was far, far deeper than its two-verse length. Jesus knew that the people were desperately searching for ultimate satisfaction. For many the search might be arduous and yet disappointing.. There would be "simulated" satisfactions; perhaps a "cultured" happiness. But the searching spirit was certainly to be commended. Hadn't Jesus Himself said, "Seek and ye shall find" (Matthew 7:7)? But when the search ends, when the "priceless," perfect pearl—the Kingdom of Heaven—is seen, and its genuineness realized, there is still a cost. It took *all* that the merchant had—everything—to obtain it. Farewell forever to the lesser! God be praised for the greater!

For a moment think of the pearl merchant not as a fictional character, but as a contemporary dealer consumed by a passion to hold in his hand the most beautiful, the most perfect, the most exquisite pearl ever seen. It has been his business to acquire "goodly" (high quality) pearls, and he will go anywhere to get them Intuitively, he knows that somewhere there *is* "the pearl of pearls." Where he goes in his search is *unmentioned.* But in imagination we see him, darting in and out of every shop, every bazaar, every auction, wherever all activity centres around the buying and selling of pearls.

The pursuit might propel him to visit Yemen's mountainous island of Socotra at the mouth of the Gulf of Aden. He has heard that from the surrounding saltwater depths there might be dredged a pearl of incomparable beauty and immense worth. Or he might work his way to the oldest pearl fisheries of all—in those rolling straits off the north coast of Sri Lanka that divide the country from the sub-continent of India. But success still eludes him. Perhaps the warm waters of Bahrain, which have produced some of the choicest pearls of all time, is at this very moment lapping the oyster shell that houses his dream. Freshwater pearls, obtainable in many parts of the world, do not interest him. They lack the iridescence that makes one pearl superior to another. Color is important. Shades may range from white through pale casts of rose, yellow, blue and green, to brown and black. The most valuable are white, cream, rose and black. Our merchant wants the best, not a second-best. So his search goes on.

He is totally uninterested in a "simulated" pearl. To the ordinary eye there may not be any appreciable difference in appearance between a cultured and a natural pearl; but to the professional, to the expert, to the merchant of the parable, artificiality cannot compete with nature. Probably he would have had scant interest in Kokichi Mikimoto, the man who, at 35 years of age, proved his University of Tokyo's professor's theory correct that when a foreign object enters a pearl oyster's shell and is not expelled, the oyster will use it as the core of a pearl. Kokichi had heard that the Chinese had been artificially inducing pearl growth for centuries, so he began to experiment. On July 11, 1893, out of a sheltered bay, Kokichi pulled up a bamboo basket for routine inspection of its contents. In one of the oysters harvested he discovered that he had actually "created" the world's first commercially viable cultured pearl. It was a beautiful specimen, but it was unnatural. The pearl merchant is not searching for a synthetic pearl that is the product of a laboratory. His search will not end until he finds the one pearl that will cost him all the pearls he has. Remarkably, once possessed, it will have no commercial value at all. It will be genuinely "priceless."

Jesus' 34-word parable leaves much *unmentioned*, and plenty to our imagination. But His allusion has introduced us to a merchant who valued quality above quantity, as should we. One great original painting is worth more than 50 reproductions. One friend is worth more than 50 boon companions. Through long experience the merchant had learned to recognize the quality of the pearls he saw. Otherwise, how would he have recognized the "perfect" pearl? If we train ourselves to recognize true values, eventually we will know the best when we see it, and love the highest when confronted by it. We shall acquire good taste, and once we have it, we will know that no price is too high to pay for the best.

John Mason was a 17th century vicar who produced one of the first volumes of hymns, a distinct departure from the metrical Psalms then used by the Church of England. He was described as "humble and obliging: his discourse of spiritual things charmed all that had any spiritual relish." Six times a day he went aside to wrestle with his Lord in prayer, and out of his private devotions came a special sweetness of words and melody. Centuries later we are still singing his personal testimony:

I've found the pearl of greatest price,
My heart doth sing for joy;
And sing I must, for Christ I have,
O what a Christ have I!
Salvation Army Song Book No. 346